Burlesque:
A LIVING HISTORY

by Jane Briggeman

Burlesque: A Living History

© 2009 Jane Briggeman

For information, address:

BearManor Media
P. O. Box 71426
Albany, GA 31708

bearmanormedia.com

Book design and layout by Valerie Thompson

Published in the USA by BearManor Media

ISBN—1-59393-469-6
978-1-59393-469-9

Table of Contents

Acknowledgments

*B*urlesque: *A Living History* was a group effort. If it were not for the continuous help and support from past and present members of The Golden Days of Burlesque Historical Society, all who were a part of old-time burlesque, and their families, there would be no stories to tell, no photos to share, and no history to preserve. I stand and applaud all of you; may the history of burlesque live forever.

Several people deserve a special thank you and should take a well-deserved bow. Without their involvement, this collection may not have stayed intact: the late Lee Stuart, Beverly Roberts, Lee Angel, Ricki Covette, La Savona, Malcolm Smith, Charles J. Lais, Darlene Larson, Ed Wendt, Lili Marlene, Sequin, Joan Torino, Lowell Smith, Taffey O'Neil and her husband Howard, the late Sunny Dare, Sandra Ellis, Floyd Vivino, Maria Bradley, and Brunie Brice.

Lastly, I want to thank my Publisher, Ben Ohmart, and the team of creative engineers at BearManor Media. Without their patience, understanding, and expertise, this book would not exist.

Dedication

To the members of The Golden Days of Burlesque Historical Society, especially those who have become "family" over the years—you know who you are, and to the many fond reunion memories we have shared together. I have enjoyed the time I've been allowed to spend in your lives, and I feel blessed to have met many wonderful people through this venture. Unfortunately many of our friends have been lost over the nearly fifteen years the group has been together, and I know we all miss them greatly. However, I also know we shall all meet again someday.

To the late Jennie Lee, who created the first Burlesque Historical Society and kept many of the old-time dancers connected before she died in 1990. Also to "Aunt Pat" Flannery, an "Irish Imp" with a loving soul; to Toni Carroll Richards who helped me connect with Val de Val shortly before she died, and her sister—for that I will be forever grateful; to Nancy Suby, a good chum and fellow "Iowegian;" and lastly to Sunny, with love and appreciation, always and forever.

An Observation from the Unpainted Side of the Scenery

BY MIKE GILMORE (THEATRE ELECTRICIAN)

Oh! How I miss when I reminisce;
the friendly ways of those by-gone days.
Poor burlesque, how the populace frowned;
at women who danced and became ungowned.

Some women played straight for they could talk;
others were proud of their regal walk.
The comics, in their own way;
tried to make their bits risqué.

In the very first row, an eager young sailor;
waited patiently for the feature's third trailer.
Burlesque has been dead for many years;
anymore to be said would lead to tears.

Introduction

In early 1995, The Golden Days of Burlesque Historical Society was created when Tanayo, "The Costa Rican Dream Girl," asked for help in finding old friends. Her objective was to reconnect with people she had known and worked with from burlesque, and to do so while she was still well. Unfortunately, in August 2003 she passed away, and the group, a legendary cast from the golden days of burlesque, continues on but fluctuates in size. Not only do we find and reconnect with those who worked in old-time burlesque (by or before 1965) but we also strive to preserve as much history as possible. Our web site can be found at: www.burlesquehistory.com. The Golden Days of Burlesque Historical Society, a 501c(3) non-profit organization, welcomes donations and reunion and individual sponsorships, as well as inquiries that are helpful in promoting the preservation of this history. We recently were approached to help provide background photos for the movie, *Burlesque.*

Preserving this information now assures that the history lives on. We also strongly disagree with those who write about performers after they die and tend to blow the truth out of proportion. Some performers, not only those who worked in burlesque, but from other stages as well, have been maligned after their deaths. To quote one of our dancers, "None of us were saints, but if people are going to describe us, I, for one, would like my memory to be preserved accurately!"

At a future time, The Golden Days of Burlesque Historical Society collection will be donated in its entirety to a university or state historical society in the hopes they will continue to preserve what we have started. It distresses us to see memorabilia tossed away by family members or friends, or sold on ebay auctions—material important to their loved ones—which should have been preserved in a collection such as ours. Many photographs in this book are one-of-a-kind. The originals disappeared when people died. In other cases, memorabilia was specifically donated to The Golden Days of Burlesque Historical Society with the intent that it be preserved for future generations to enjoy and study. I only wish that had happened with everyone we have lost over the years.

The entire history of burlesque is impossible to contain in a single book. For additional reading, refer to my first book, *Burlesque: Legendary Stars of the Stage. Burlesque: A Living History* covers many additional bits and pieces about old-time burlesque. Those of us involved in the creation of this book hopes the public enjoys it. If interested in The Golden Days of Burlesque Historical Society or burlesque history in general, please contact us through our publisher or web site.

A Legendary Cast from the Golden Days of Burlesque

"Class" best describes members of The Golden Days of Burlesque Historical Society. You are invited to meet just a few who worked in old-time burlesque and have become a part of this organization. This chapter does not include everyone who is or was a part of the group. However, a list of all our members, both past and present at the time of publication, is included at the end of this book.

SHAWNA ST. CLAIR

Miss St. Clair was an original member of The Golden Days of Burlesque Historical Society. Shawna once explained what she thought made a good striptease dancer in burlesque: "The burlesque queen did her act well if she had been sexy but not vulgar, seductive but not lewd, pleasing but not offensive; she must be a real temptress with class. Tease—that was the name of the game." Also performing under the names Dixie Dae and Ginger Woods, Shawna retired in 1972, and in 1997, she passed away.

AL BAKER, JR.

He is the son of a straight man, Al Baker, Sr., and burlesque dancer/talking woman, Marcella. Young Al began his career in burlesque theatres at the age of twelve, when he briefly worked as a candy butcher. In 1958 at the age of twenty-four, Junior leased his first theatre, the State Theatre in Canton, Ohio. From there, he proceeded to own twenty-two burlesque theatres across the country including the Troc in Philadelphia, and the Mayfair in New York City, as well as some legitimate nightclubs.

Shawna St. Clair. PHOTO COURTESY OF: MARINKA.

AMBER MIST

In 1964, Amber was tending a bar in South Miami. A retired dancer from New Orleans suggested she become an exotic dancer. Agent Sammy Clark signed her on and then booked her as a co-feature at the Buccaneer Lounge, where she perfected her act for three months before touring clubs and the last remaining burlesque theatres, which she preferred. Introduced as "Beautiful Amber Mist, Miss Burlesque, Herself," she was known for performing

Val Valentine and Al Baker, Jr. in front of the Mayfair Theatre, October 1967.
PHOTO COURTESY OF: AL BAKER, JR.

a contortionist act, which required doing vast amounts of floor work. However, Amber had previously studied ballet, tap, toe-tap, and acrobatic dancing for fifteen years. Toe-tap is considered to be a lost art, and Amber hopes to see it revived.

Various routines she performed in her act included: a street scene, gay nineties, a bride left at the altar, a flapper dancing the Charleston, fan dance, a bathtub scene, and an act that required an old purple velvet chaise lounge. Amber always wore two g-strings, so if audiences thought they saw something, they did not. After returning from another Midwest tour, she played in Jacksonville, Florida, where she fell in love with club owner Jimmie Bryan, whose wife had recently passed away. Jimmie began his career decades earlier by performing for the Billy Rose Circus as a gymnast tumbling on an elephant's back. He also worked the vaudeville circuit and on occasion worked with Jimmy Durante.

In the late 1930s, Jimmie bought his first club, and then went on to own several clubs in the Jacksonville area including: Dutch Mill, Forest Inn, Candy Cane, Foxie Lady, the Tabu Club, and the Skyway Club, which had originally been owned by his father, Baker Bryan. Jimmie and Amber were happily married until his death in 1981, when Amber returned to school and earned an advanced college degree. Amber Mist's publicity material, including photos, ads, and clippings from when she worked as an exotic dancer, have all been lost or destroyed, but we hope they can be replaced.

ANN PETT

At the age of five, Ann remembered standing on a chair to reach the needle on the phonograph player, as she learned to sing her first Slovenian songs. By age seven, she was appearing on stage with the Slovene National Benefit Society, and as a teenager Ann was second runner-up in the Miss St. Louis beauty contest. Ann spent a summer traveling with a woman's baseball team, and she was equally excited to be the only girl on an all-male baseball team. Then, Ann left home and joined the Mardell Dancers as an actress/chorus girl in a mini-musical covering forty theatres throughout the south.

Upon reaching New York, she worked by day for millionaire Fortune Pope, who owned radio station WHOM. At night, she rehearsed dance routines for gangster Mickey Cohen. Ann was startled to learn that those marvelous dances were to be performed in shows in a chain of burlesque theatres throughout the East coast. The shows included beautiful girls, costumes, a live orchestra, and famous comics. In the late 1950s after touring the circuit, she returned to New York City for additional training in voice, dance, and acting. She auditioned for an Italian choreographer and producer, who promoted a road show across the United States which featured her as, Ann Pett, "The Cosmopolitan Girl." Ann also worked for Harold Minsky, choreographer and theatrical agent Dick Richards, and she had a long run in Ann Corio's show, *This Was Burlesque*, as well as in Sol Richman Productions featuring Mickey Hargitay and comic Frank Silvano.

Ann wrote, "There was always a competitive streak to have gimmicks. That lead me to my chic-to-chic daring cut-out at the derriere, on the long svelte sequined gowns I wore, which incited wonderful laughter as I danced at countless engagements in New York City trophy hotel ballrooms such as the Waldorf Astoria, the Plaza, and the Statler, which were always filled with Wall Street financiers. My jeweled g-string always remained intact. During one engagement, a pink-beaded feather boa vanished, and my theatrical agent, Joe Williams, was very annoyed that I wrote post cards to all the downtown New York City corporations trying to retrieve the sparkling specialty wardrobe piece. We, and by that I mean, playfully elegant exotic dancers mostly from the East coast such as, Val Chessy, Toni Carroll, Penny Powers, Saja Lee, Anita Ventura, Barbara Carroll, Goldilocks, and Sally the Shape, often performed at fabulous hotel clubs. I always wore a hat on stage. My favorite hat was made by Jacks of Hollywood. I still have sets of fancy bra and panties that a millionaire from Maine sent. He wanted to know if my songwriter-husband would take $3 million so he could marry me. Distinctive gentlemen saw dancers on stage and frequently proposed to the young, pretty, exotic dancers. A renowned international theatrical agent, Hans Walter, asked to book me to England, Germany, and then on to Japan, but one had to flash the g-string. That was a no-no for me, so I never booked in foreign countries. My most recent performance was at the 2006 Reunion for The Burlesque Historical Society at the Stardust Hotel in Las Vegas."

Ann Pett. PHOTO COURTESY OF: BURLESQUE HISTORICAL SOCIETY.

In the last few phone calls I have received from Ann, she stressed the importance of remembering the many agents that helped the women in burlesque, most notably those who worked on the East coast. Included in this list are just some of the men she wanted burlesque fans and historians to remember: Billy Claire, Eddie Kaplan, Harry Stone, and Dave Cohan. All of them worked out of the Palace Theatre Building in New York City. Also there was Joe Williams, Irving Charnoff, John Lastfogel, Joe Blue, Aaron Toder, and her home town favorite, Mike Riaff, from St. Louis.

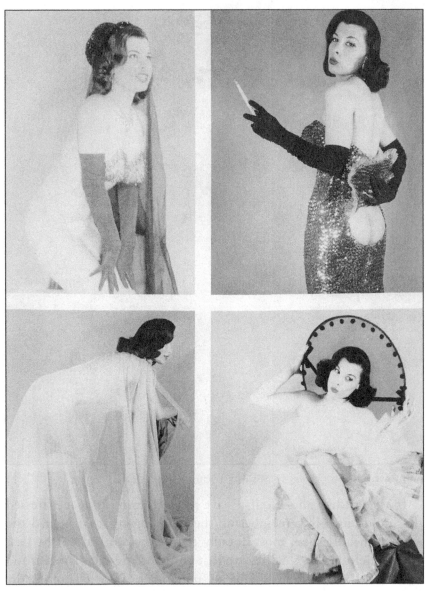

Ann Pett. PHOTO COURTESY OF: BURLESQUE HISTORICAL SOCIETY.

Ann Pett with Jackie Gleason. PHOTO COURTESY OF: ANN PETT.

Frank Silvano and Count Gregory.
PHOTO COURTESY OF: ANN PETT.

Penny Powers.
PHOTO COURTESY OF: ANN PETT.

APRIL MARCH

Billed as "The First Lady of Burlesque," April March worked in burlesque, performing across the United States, Canada, Mexico, and England, from 1952 to 1978. She headlined in two Harold Minsky Shows, as well as in Ann Corio's show, *This Was Burlesque*, for six weeks. It was during a press conference thrown by Corio that a magazine editor discovered April to be a talented golfer. Because of that interview, she became the first exotic dancer from burlesque to be given a full write-up in *Sports Illustrated*. In 1964, she appeared in *Time Piece*, a short film by Jim Henson, which won major awards within the film industry. April always preferred working theatres to clubs, and truly enjoyed getting to know all the great comics.

ATHENA

Originally billed as Marietta Del Rio, "The Latin Peeler," Athena came from Puerto Rico and worked in burlesque clubs all across the United States.

BAMBI SR.

Bambi performed as Dolores Rozelle, Bambi Brooks, Bambi Jones, and Joi Naymith. From 1949 to the 1970s, she appeared on burlesque stages throughout the United States, Canada, Mexico, and South America. Her daughter, Bambi Jr., briefly followed in her footsteps as an exotic dancer. Dori, as she is known to her friends, has written her own book, *My Journey Burlesque: The Way it Was*, which is available from RoseDog Books. It's a good book for those wanting a taste of what life was like for a woman working in burlesque during its last decades. The book also discusses her marriage to burlesque comic Artie Brooks. I believe her own words tell her story better than I ever could.

Bambi has been an extremely supportive member of The Golden Days of Burlesque Historical Society. She attends the reunions and never wants to leave. Her stories are amusing and always entertaining, but her enthusiasm to preserve what remains of this history is just part of what makes her so much fun to be around. Even though I was only lucky enough to attend a couple of gatherings held at her former home, the "Gypsy Love Ranch" in Las Vegas, they were memorable. We never knew who would show up.

Marietta Del Rio, who later performed as Athena.
PHOTO COURTESY OF: MARIETTA DEL RIO.

Marietta Del Rio.
PHOTO COURTESY OF: MARIETTA DEL RIO.

In 1999 at the Imperial Palace reunion in Las Vegas, I told Bambi that once Val de Val was found, The Golden Days of Burlesque Historical Society would be no more. I will never forget the look on her face. Not knowing me very well at the time, she thought I was serious. Rest assured, the Burlesque Historical Society will continue on as long as we have a single surviving member.

BARBARA CURTIS

Barbara, billed as "The Proper Bostonian," performed a lovely dance routine. She was married to comic Al Anger, and was known for being one of the best talking women in burlesque. For years, Barbara worked scenes with Al. After his death in 1967, she continued working scenes with other comics. Fellow performer, the late Peter "Sonny" Thomas, once wrote, "Barbara Curtis was such a talented talking woman. Every word could be heard clear as a bell in the top balcony. Audiences just loved her." Al Anger was a first cousin to the Marx Brothers, and Harry, his brother, was one of the most respected agents in New York City.

Barbara Curtis and Al Anger, 1958.
PHOTO COURTESY OF: BARBARA CURTIS AND JONI TAYLOR.

Barbara Curtis. PHOTO COURTESY OF: JONI TAYLOR.

BETTY BRIGGS

Betty was billed as "The Zebra Girl." In the 1940s and 1950s, she worked mostly in chorus lines in the Los Angeles area burlesque theatres. When asked, she would step out of the line for the extra $5-$10 and work as a strip. She also occasionally worked as an exotic dancer in local clubs, but retired after getting married. Later, Betty worked as an extra in films and television. She came to all our California reunions and was a great help by slapping nametags on everyone as they walked in the door. Betty Briggs died in 2000.

Betty Briggs.
AUTHORS COLLECTION.

BETTY ROWLAND

Billed as burlesque's "Ball of Fire," Betty is an original member of The Golden Days of Burlesque Historical Society. She is also one of the founding members of the League of Exotic Dancers (EDL), which was founded in 1955 by Jennie Lee. The EDL became an independent organization within the American Guild of Variety Artists, through which all the dancers were booked, and it dealt with a number of situations and complaints over the years.

Betty was born in Columbus, Ohio. She, Dian and Rozell, her two sisters, took dancing lessons as children and all caught the performance bug. Betty and Rozell eventually toured in vaudeville as a sister act, and then worked in Minsky's shows on Broadway in New York City. Rozell also performed at the Paradise Club, where she became known as the "Golden Girl." Later, she traveled to London, England, to perform at the Dorchester Hotel. On that first trip abroad, she met Baron Empain of Belgium, married, and then retired from performing. In 1945, Dian, who had become quite popular as a performer on her own, died from a pre-existing heart condition while appearing in a Detroit nightclub.

Betty's experience working in vaudeville helped her make the transition into burlesque, where she developed her own signature act and became a featured performer. As the "Ball of Fire," Betty danced to the song "In the Mood," as she elegantly flowed with grace and agility on various burlesque stages all across the United States. She could also be compared to a whirling dervish, depending on the routine she performed. Betty loved to dance, and she continued to do so into the early 1960s. Not only was she a fan favorite, but all who worked with her loved her as well. Both on and off stage, Betty maintained friendships with great burlesque performers such as Gypsy Rose Lee and Lili St. Cyr.

ABOVE AND RIGHT:
Betty Rowland.
PHOTOS COURTESY OF: BETTY ROWLAND.

Betty Rowland. PHOTO COURTESY OF: BETTY ROWLAND.

Betty Rowland.
PHOTO COURTESY OF:
BURLESQUE HISTORICAL
SOCIETY.

Betty Rowland.
PHOTO COURTESY OF:
BETTY ROWLAND.

Over the years, members of the League of Exotic Dancers turned the group into a social club for the retiring dancers from burlesque. In 1990, Jennie Lee, the woman who had kept everyone connected, died, and the dancers began to drift apart. In 1995, Betty was instrumental in helping reconnect some burlesque performers in the Los Angeles area. Reunions were held for The Golden Days of Burlesque Historical Society at 217, the club Betty co-owned in Santa Monica, California. Everyone attending those events had a great time, due largely to Betty's energy, enthusiasm, and kindness. Betty Rowland will always be a "Ball of Fire."

CARMELA

She was billed as "The Sophia Loren of Burlesque," and grew up in Washington, D.C. While working as a waitress, Carmela also attended dancing school. "I was never a good student. I had to do my own thing my own way," Carmela said. However, not long after that, she began dancing in burlesque clubs in the Washington, D.C. area. She was a self-taught dancer. At the time, Carmela was twenty years old and a divorced mother of two.

Agent Sol Goodman eventually signed Carmela to a contract, and from 1950 to 1976, she performed all over the United States. She preferred burlesque theatres to clubs. She also worked in Europe, Canada, and South America, often following Tempest Storm, or co-featuring with Blaze Starr.

"Sol booked Blaze Starr, who was a leading girl at the time," she said. "He had a number of great, wonderful girls working for him at that time. I wanted to be one of those girls."

Other performers with whom Carmela worked included: Louis Armstrong, Soupie Sales, and Don Rickles. She is especially proud of the performance she gave for President Kennedy's honor guard.

When she began dancing in burlesque, Carmela was billed as "Carmela the Torrid Twister," but Goodman encouraged her to change her stage name to "Carmela, the Sophia Loren of Burlesque." With more experience, Carmela learned to put together better dance routines by watching other dancers and combining the best aspects of what they did into her own show. "I did a lot of muscle control, quivers, deep back bends, and acrobatic stuff like splits and head spins. I had hair down to my butt and colored it cherry red, so when I spun my head around, it looked like fire. I also did a lot of comedy. I loved to talk to the audience."

Between shows, Carmela stayed in her dressing room and created her own costumes. "Every sequin, every bead, and every jewel had to be individually sewn on by hand. I used plastic beads because crystal beads would cut the thread." She started making her own costumes because prices for pre-made costumes were astronomical. At the time, just the bra and panties of a burlesque gown cost as much as $200. Once she learned to do the bead work, making costumes was easy. Elaborate gowns took weeks, and simpler designs took far less time.

In 1976, Carmela moved from the east to Las Vegas. One to not mince words, she was always quick to state that today's clubs and young dancers never impressed her. "When I was working men were not allowed to touch the dancers. There were bouncers around who made sure of that. During the era I performed, in most cases, the audience's were great. It was fun and exciting. We got to meet a lot of wonderful people. I'm proud of my career in old-time burlesque."

Carmela also took great pride in her Italian/Spanish heritage. In 1700, a Spanish ancestor named Torregrossa went to Italy, where the King and Queen presented him with the title of Marquis. Carmela explained, "This is how the Torregrossa name got its start in Italy." Carmela, "The Sophia Loren of Burlesque," passed away on January 11th, 2008.

Carmela, The Sophia Loren of Burlesque.
PHOTO COURTESY OF: CARMELA RICKMAN.

Carmela, The Sophia Loren of Burlesque. PHOTO COURTESY OF: AL BAKER, JR.

Carmela, The Sophia Loren of Burlesque. PHOTO COURTESY OF: CARMELA RICKMAN.

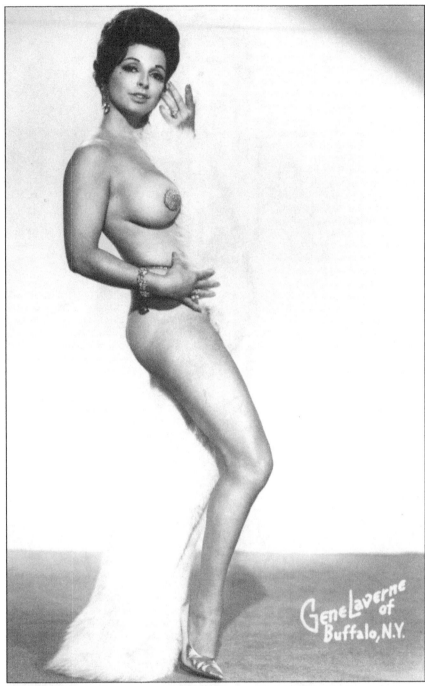

Carmela, The Sophia Loren of Burlesque.
PHOTO COURTESY OF: CARMELA RICKMAN.

CHASTIDY JONES

Billed as "Venus with Arms," Chastidy worked in burlesque for more than twenty years. She worked for Jess Mack and with Sally Rand, Liz Lyons, Sue Martin, and Shalimar.

CONNIE MERCEDES

From 1950 to 1988, Connie worked in burlesque, including performances in the Ann Corio show, *This Was Burlesque*. She also danced on Broadway, as well as throughout the United States, Canada, England, Europe, Mexico, and Japan.

CYNTHIANA

From 1963 to 1970, Cynthiana danced in burlesque clubs and theatres. She mostly worked on the West coast, Hawaii, and Japan, but was particularly popular in Louisville, Kentucky. She was known for the large hats she wore in her routines, which were all made by Kiva.

Cynthiana.
AUTHORS COLLECTION.

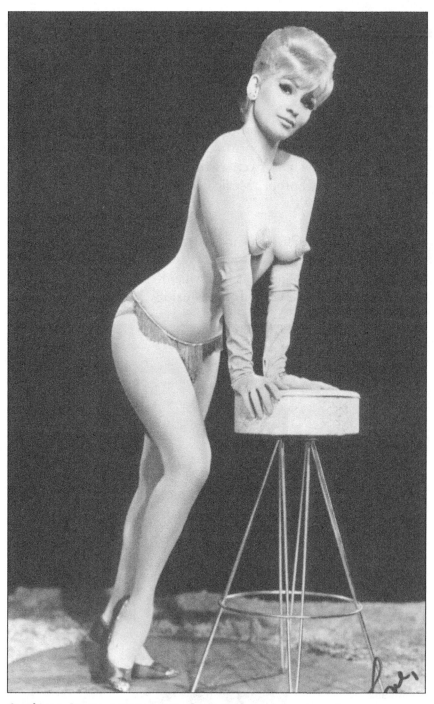

Cynthiana. PHOTO COURTESY OF: CYNTHIANA.

Daphne Lake

Born and raised in Buffalo, New York, Daphne began her show business career in 1963 by working in a carnival sideshow. She was hired to perform as a knife-thrower's assistant, but due to his passion for alcohol, she felt more like his target. Daphne quickly became the new snake charmer in the show for a short time, and then she took a job as a "Bally Girl" in a girl's show.

Daphne wrote, "The show hired some of us as "extras" so they could pull people into the actual show. As a "Bally Girl," I never stripped, but I got to know the acts, realized that they were working a whole lot less than me, and they made more money. Plus, I liked the costumes, feathers, chiffon, and satin. Everything was on the up-and-up. There were no extra privileges for the customers and no total nudity. When it got to the end of the season, the dancers were even wearing full-body leotards under their g-strings and net-bras because it was so cold."

While the carnival wintered in Gibsonton, Florida, Daphne spotted a newspaper ad for a theatre in St. Petersburg that was looking for dancers. They paid $75 a week. She made the trip, applied for the job, and got hired. The theatre, one of three created and owned by the Kaplan family, was part of a mini-circuit consisting of theatres in St. Petersburg, and Pensacola, Florida, as well as Pittsburgh, Pennsylvania. Using the name "Jezebelle," she performed in three shows a day, seven days a week, and worked one month at each theatre. They even provided used costumes for the new girls to borrow and buy on time out of their salaries, if they chose. Daphne thought she was in heaven. By 1970, she was a featured performer, billed as "Daphne Lake." She created routines that revolved around the use of fire, marshmallows, or feathers.

Daphne wrote, "Owners were demanding favors, and there were more and more porn shows in the clubs. They placed more importance on how many bottles of champagne we conned the customers into buying than how glamorous our wardrobe was, or that we could even do a dance with fire. I couldn't work that way, so I just gave up. Theatres were almost all gone, and the ones that remained were doing really hard-core porn revues. I did my last show on a Saturday, and then I went to work in an office the very next Monday. I worked with a lot of the older girls in the theatres. Many had started dancing at the age of fourteen, and they knew little else. I realized I wasn't going to be able to support myself in burlesque, so as I got older, I kept up on my education."

Knowing I enjoy hearing about the old theatres, Daphne shared the following story:

"I cried when I heard that the Roxy Theatre in Cleveland was torn down. I was only there one week, but I felt I was a part of its history. The walls at stage right were old, black stone blocks, and they were from three to five feet high. They were covered in old, solidified chewing gum. I felt that the chorus girls must have stuck their gum there just before going on stage so many decades before back when they did six shows a day. I always wanted to look through the basement or attic to see what treasures were to be found. When I did the last show of the night, very few people were left backstage, and I was truly afraid to go exploring on my own. In those days, there were no more chorus lines, and I could feel the ghosts coming out to roam their home. It was the only theatre I ever worked that had the semi-circle runway enclosing the orchestra pit. It was right out of old vaudeville!"

Billed as "Miss Elegance," Daphne Lake never worked the West coast, but she did perform in theatres and clubs on the East coast, in the Midwest, in the southern United States, and also in Canada. In 1973, she retired from dancing.

Daphne Lake. PHOTO COURTESY OF: DAPHNE LAKE.

A variety of clippings promoting Daphne Lake's performances across the country.
PHOTO COURTESY OF: DAPHNE LAKE.

Daphne Lake, who began her career as Jezebelle.
PHOTO COURTESY OF: DAPHNE LAKE.

More clippings promoting Daphne Lake's performances across the country.
PHOTO COURTESY OF: DAPHNE LAKE.

A photo taken under the name of Jezebelle.
PHOTO COURTESY OF: DAPHNE LAKE.

Daphne Lake. PHOTO COURTESY OF: DAPHNE LAKE.

Darlene Larson

In the late 1960s, Darlene appeared in *Minsky's Burlesque Follies*. At that time, burlesque shows still had chorus lines, as well as exotics, baggy pants comedians, and variety acts. Performing as a showgirl in the chorus line, she toured with the show throughout the United States. She also worked for Dick Richards, (not the comic), in *The New Look of Burlesque*, appearing at club dates around the New York City area. In Dick's show, she performed as a showgirl and talking woman. Darlene always said that was her favorite show because it gave her a chance to act in skits and wear glamorous costumes in the chorus line.

Appearing at the Latin Quarter in New York City, 1967.
Photo courtesy of: Darlene Larson.

DEE MILO

Billed as the "Venus of Dance," Dee Milo performed in burlesque theatres and clubs across the United States, Japan, and Mexico, from 1949 to 1964. She also toured in USO Shows. In 1957 while working in Mexico, she met Jennie Lee. They remained close friends until Jennie's death. Dee, known for her "Sentimental Journey" number, nearly went to jail when she introduced a new routine called, "I Married an Angel." Upon retiring from burlesque, all related memorabilia, including photos, publicity, and costumes, was burned in a fire. For more than forty years, Dee has been involved in the healing arts community, including the practice of energy healing. She is also the creator of the CDR Balancer (www.deemilo.com), and is always willing to perform an exotic dance number when asked.

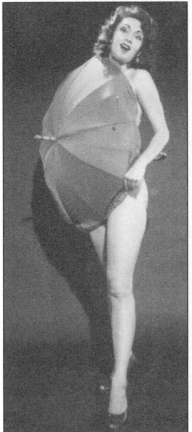

A very young Dee Milo, Venus of Dance.
PHOTOS COURTESY OF: DEE MILO.

Dee Milo backstage preparing to perform. PHOTO COURTESY OF: DEE MILO.

Work card provided giving Dee Milo permission to live and perform in Mexico.
PHOTO COURTESY OF: DEE MILO.

A young Dee Milo posing in her red gown. PHOTO COURTESY OF: DEE MILO.

Dee Milo, as she appeared in 1995, wearing the same red gown—the only gown saved from "a ritualistic burning."
PHOTO COURTESY OF: DEE MILO AND EARL HANSEN.

DELILAH JONES

Before her career in burlesque, Delilah worked as a pin-up model, appearing in over seventy-five magazines as "Doris Gohlke." In 1955, she was crowned Miss Teenage Berlin, and in 1957, she was the second runner up in the Miss Germany Pageant.

In 1959, Delilah began dancing in burlesque clubs in the Los Angeles area. Both Sally Rand and Tempest Storm worked with Delilah, helping her learn the fine art of performing with fans and providing suggestions for her act. She specialized in belly dancing and contortionist routines, as well as performing in a large champagne glass. Delilah regularly appeared at the world famous Palomino Club in Las Vegas, and she also worked all over the United States, Canada, and Mexico. In the late 1970s, she retired from burlesque and worked in several movies and television shows.

Delilah Jones. PHOTO COURTESY OF: DELILAH JONES.

LEFT AND BELOW:
Delilah Jones.
PHOTOS COURTESY OF:
DELILAH JONES.

DIANE DE LYS

From 1938 to 1948, Diane performed as a specialty dancer, using the name "Diane Page." From 1948 to 1969 she performed as Diane De Lys. She worked all over Europe before returning to the United States at the start of World War Two. She loved dancing in both clubs and theatres. However, her contracts stated that she could not mix with customers when working in clubs. "The Devil and the Virgin" was one of her best-known routines.

ELECTRA

This tiny woman stood just over five feet tall. During the first six years of her burlesque career, she toured with an electric light outfit routine. Later, Electra changed her act and began impersonating Mae West—something she did until her death. According to Electra, she and Gypsy Rose Lee maintained a feud for decades. Early in their careers, comic Rags Ragland chose Electra as his talking woman for a scene that Gypsy wanted to do. Electra died in 1999.

Electra. PHOTO COURTESY OF: LERI VALE.

THE FASCINATING JENNIFER

In 1954 when the Casino Burlesque Theatre in Boston re-opened, Jennifer was invited to dance in the chorus line. After learning stage presence, she was asked to do a solo striptease routine, which was of no interest to the young dancer until after Sequin came to the theatre and performed. Watching Sequin's routine, which contained no bumps and grinds, Jennifer began creating her own costumes and routines, and she frequently filled-in on stage when needed. In 1957, "The Fascinating Jennifer" toured on the Bryan & Engle circuit as a co-feature. By 1958, she was performing as a feature, continuing to work in burlesque theatres until her retirement in 1963.

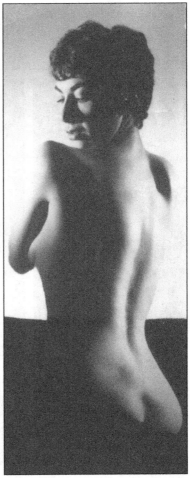

The Fascinating Jennifer.
PHOTOS COURTESY OF: THE
FASCINATING JENNIFER.

ABOVE AND RIGHT:
The Fascinating Jennifer.
PHOTOS COURTESY OF: THE
FASCINATING JENNIFER

Just some members of the 1954 Boston Casino Theatre chorus line. Jennifer, front and center.
PHOTO COURTESY OF: THE FASCINATING JENNIFER.

The Fascinating Jennifer.
PHOTO COURTESY OF: BURLESQUE HISTORICAL SOCIETY

FRANKIE RAY

Also known as Frank Ray Perilli, Frankie Ray began his career as a nightclub comic. For several years, he co-starred with pal Shecky Green at the Wits End Club in New Orleans. When Green signed a contract to work on the Colgate Comedy Hour television show, Frankie also came to Hollywood to work as a writer for the program. In addition to creating material for Green, he also wrote for Dean Martin and Don Rickles. His other projects included writing movie scripts, producing, and working as an emcee in burlesque. He is very proud to have written the European cult film, *The Doberman Gang*, with Lou Garfinkle, a business partner of twenty-five years. Frankie and Lenny Bruce were also close friends, so when it came

Frankie Ray. PHOTO COURTESY OF: FRANKIE RAY.

time for me to find Sally Marr, also known as "Boots Malloy," Frankie Ray helped out immensely. He and I met at the very first reunion for the Burlesque Historical Society in 1995, and it was love at first sight, at least for me.

Frankie Ray.
PHOTO COURTESY OF: FRANKIE RAY.

GILDA AND HER CROWNING GLORY

Gilda was also known as "Shirley Jean" in the Our Gang/Little Rascals movies. In-between movie jobs, she began her burlesque career as a chorus girl at the Follies Theatre in Los Angeles. Her last film job was as a dancer in *Singing in the Rain*. Lillian Hunt, choreographer at the Follies, gave Gilda her first job as a striptease dancer and talking woman, and then went on to manage her career in burlesque. Known for her waist-long, golden hair, Gilda was voted #9 on the All-Time Best Strips list by Jennie Lee's Exotic Dancers League. During her career, Gilda worked theatres and clubs all over the United States and Canada. In the late 1950s, she retired. Gilda died in February 2009.

Gilda. AUTHORS COLLECTION.

Gilda. Photo courtesy of: Gussie Gross/Burlesque Historical Society.

GINA BON BON

Gina was born in Cuba, and in 1965, she began her burlesque career dancing in the chorus line at the Latin Quarter Club in New York City. Soon after, she was featuring on the burlesque circuit for Al Baker Jr., appearing in clubs and theatres all over the United States, Canada, and Guam. Gina worked for big name burlesque agents Jess Mack, Dick Richards, and Ross Russell. She worked in the *Minsky's Follies*, at the Playboy Club, and in *Burlesque USA*, which starred Red Buttons and Robert Alda. That show ran in theatres all across the United States and Canada. In 1980, HBO filmed the show. She also performed in many clubs, including: The Cabaret in Las Vegas, and The Penthouse in Vancouver, Canada. While headlining in a burlesque revue in Pennsylvania she landed the first of several film roles—a cameo in *Going Home*, which starred Robert Mitchum, Brenda Vaccaro, and Jan-Michael Vincent. In 1990, after giving her final live performance in Hawaii, Gina retired from dancing and went on to work in television and films, including *Fever Pitch*, which starred Ryan O'Neal.

Gina Bon Bon. PHOTO COURTESY OF: GINA BON

GUSSIE GROSS

Gussie was a wardrobe and costume-maker for many dancers performing in burlesque theatres and clubs, mostly on the West coast. She was introduced to burlesque by her first husband, a policeman, when he raided the Follies Theatre in Los Angeles. The choreographer at the Follies Theatre learned of her skills as a seamstress and hired Gussie and her cousin to design and sew costumes, pasties, and g-strings for the chorus line and house strips. The two women went on to create costumes for individual feature performers for several decades. In May 2006, Gussie passed away.

HONEY STANDISH

Honey was born in Kansas and raised in Texas. She is a rancher's daughter and an eleventh descendent of Captain Myles Standish, who escorted the Pilgrims to America in 1620. In 1944, Honey started her career as a performer in circuses and carnivals. She quickly turned to working on the burlesque stage as a chorus line dancer. She performed from 1945 to 1949 solely at the old Rialto Theatre in Chicago. She told me, "I was the one who led the chorus line on and off stage." Her real love was art. The traveling Honey did in her youth allowed her to study art with various private teachers and in many museums, galleries, and libraries. Since 1954, she has resided in the Detroit area. In 1959, she created the La Belle Miel Art School, a private school for children and adults. Honey demonstrated and taught students in all media including painting, charcoal, ceramics, and free-form sculpture. She also taught classes in art theory and art history. Honey, as well as several of her students, won many awards in a variety of Michigan art shows. Garden Art Shows were also held every summer in Honey's own backyard. In addition to her numerous one-woman shows, Honey was invited to hang her artwork at a number of prestigious shows and galleries, including Macomb Art Society, Michigan Art Education Association, National Art Education Association, Lakeside Palette Club, Women's Caucus for Art, Detroit Institute of Art, Toledo Art Museum, and the Chicago Art Institute.

Irving Benson

Irving was twenty-one years old when he first set foot on a burlesque stage. He soon became one of the youngest featured comics. Irving worked as a "top banana" all over the country, performing as Harold Minsky's principal comic for more than thirty years.

Jimmy Mathews

Jimmy began his career more than seventy years ago, and there is not a burlesque stage in the United States where he did not perform. Before Lee Stuart died, he heard of Jimmy's death and shared the following story:

"First time I met Jim was in 1949. I was twenty-one and he was thirty-seven and one of the younger comics. He and I became friends because I played the fiddle and he played the banjo, so between shows, we'd jam in the basement. Later, Ray Kolb told me a story about Jimmy that traveled around the circuit. It seems that when Jimmy was young, nice-looking, and the third banana on a three-comic bill, the other two comics were old men with no teeth when performing on stage. Try as he might, Jim could not get a laugh in the scenes. One day, he asked the older guys why he wasn't getting any laughs, and they both simultaneously said, 'Hell Boy, you got teeth.' They were kidding, of course, but Jim took it seriously. The next day, he went down the street to a dentist. I believe they were in San Francisco. Jim got in the chair and the dentist asked, 'Mr. Mathews what can I do for you?' Jim replied, 'You can pull my teeth.' The dentist told Jimmy he couldn't pull a perfect set of teeth and asked why in the world would he ask such a thing anyway. Well, I'm not sure if Jim talked this dentist into doing it, or found another dentist who would, but his answer was, 'I'm a burlesque comic and the other guys are getting all the laughs.' Bottom line is, he had a good set of teeth pulled in one day and began getting laughs."

Jimmy performed in Ann Corio's long-running revue, *This Was Burlesque*, and in many Minsky shows. For three and a half years, he also worked in *Sugar Babies* with Mickey Rooney and Ann Miller. Jimmy Mathews shared the stage with many famous comedians, including Joe Yule Sr., Mickey Rooney's father, and spent more than forty years working with straight man,

Jimmy Mathews.
PHOTO COURTESY OF:
PAT ELLIOTT
MINSKY/BURLESQUE
HISTORICAL SOCIETY.

Dexter Maitland. He was one of the most-admired performers from burlesque. In October 2004, he passed away at the age of ninety-one.

JOAN ARLINE

From 1954 to 1959, Joan was known as the "The Sexquire Girl." She worked in burlesque throughout the Midwest and East coast. For the first three months of her career, she worked under the name of "Rudya Ray," until house singer Paul West suggested she use her real name, Joan Arline. Soon after, Dewey Michaels, owner of the Palace Theatre in Buffalo, New York reported to Milt Schuster that Joan was "feature material." From then on, she was a headliner on the burlesque circuit, as well as in nightclubs. Known mostly for an act that included two white Russian Wolfhounds, she was billed as "Joan Arline, The Sexquire Girl and her Royal Escorts." Joan was also famous for her routine called "The Seven Approaches of a Man," which she still performs today in her one-woman show.

Regarding her early burlesque experiences, Joan wrote, "I worked in the bits in my first year on the circuit. I had done a great deal of acting as a teenager in Connecticut in various community theatre productions. I knew how to project, so a few of the comics liked me. My favorite comic was Harry Clexx. I also enjoyed working with Scurvy Miller at the Gayety Theatre in Detroit. He was a sweet man. I also worked with straight man Dexter Maitland, and of course, Paul West. Dexter and Paul were later with Ann Corio in *This Was Burlesque*. I worked with Herbie Faye, as well as Sammy Price. Sammy used to bring rye bread, onions, and limburger cheese for the entire company to enjoy before the midnight show every Saturday night. On Sunday, the theatre still stunk. It was funny to see the audience as they entered, twitching their noses and trying to figure out what that smell was. I have always been grateful for the comedy timing I learned in burlesque."

Joan went on to write, "I always did a classy act—dancing and a great deal of teasing—not many bumps and grinds. I used the right music for certain choreographed moves, but my act was not completely choreographed at all times. I worked off the audience a lot. I never had much of a chance to watch other dancers. I don't think I patterned my work after anyone. I wasn't a fringe shaker, a tassel twirler, or a spinner. I often moved to the audience responses and what I could feel from them."

In recent years, Joan Arline has run her own dance studio in Detroit. She appeared with the *Palm Springs Follies*, as well as performed vintage strip routines and acted in a variety of shows in Atlantic City, Palm Springs, and Las Vegas. Her mother used to say, "I can't believe it; all that ballet and she goes into burlesque." Her father responded, "At least they both begin with the letter 'B.'"

ABOVE LEFT:
Joan Arline, "The Sexquire Girl and her Royal Escorts."
PHOTO COURTESY OF: JOAN ARLINE.

ABOVE RIGHT:
Joan Arline, "The Sexquire Girl."
PHOTO COURTESY OF: JOAN ARLINE.

LEFT:
Joan Arline, "The Sexquire Girl."
PHOTO COURTESY OF: JOAN ARLINE.

Joan Arline and Scury Miller performing together in a comedy bit in 1955 at the Gayety Theatre in Detroit, Michigan.
PHOTO COURTESY OF: JOAN ARLINE.

Joan enjoyed working scenes when asked; Scurvy Miller was a favorite.
PHOTO COURTESY OF: JOAN ARLINE.

Help us identify this straight man appearing with Joan Arline and Scurvy Miller.
PHOTO COURTESY OF: JOAN ARLINE.

JONI TAYLOR

In 1952, Joni began her career working in the chorus line at the Casino Theatre in Pittsburgh. Comic George Murray was the theatre manager, and his wife, Eileen Hubert, a former dancer and talking woman, choreographed the shows. As her career progressed, Joni went on the road, working in bits with comic Charlie Robinson and dancing as a co-feature. She always worked in theatres on the East coast. She performed as a pretty, young dancer, or she blackened her teeth and played the hausfrau in comedy scenes. No matter the situation, she was always adaptable. In 1964, Joni left burlesque, but filled-in when AGVA called for a last-minute replacement. She was proud to have worked with many top-notch comics and straight men from the last decades of burlesque, but Joni Taylor also just loved to dance.

Joni Taylor.
PHOTO COURTESY OF: JONI TAYLOR.

Joni Taylor, 1957.
PHOTO COURTESY OF:JONI TAYLOR.

BELOW:
Joni Taylor, 1959.
PHOTO COURTESY OF:
JONI TAYLOR.

RIGHT:
Joni Taylor.
PHOTO COURTESY OF:
JONI TAYLOR.

K.C. LAYNE

It was in the mid-1960s, just as the last theatres were closing and good acts were performing in supper clubs, that K.C. began dancing. In those days she was known as "Joani Layne."

K. C. wrote, "People said I looked like the Playboy Mascot and performed like Rose La Rose. I worked mostly in the Midwest in wonderful clubs like The Gay 90s, T-Bone Club, Rainbow Room, Blue Note, Tip's, and the Black Poodle. I had the pleasure of working with many beautiful, bright, funny, and talented performers. All I can say is thank you to all the big stars, little stars, bright stars, and fading stars, and what a hell of a good time we had."

Upon retiring from burlesque, K. C. worked in films and promos, and later became an accountant. She paints, has art work hanging in galleries, and plans to hold a one-woman show in the future.

K. C. Layne.
PHOTO COURTESY OF: K. C. LAYNE.

K. C. Layne.
Photo courtesy of: K. C. Layne.

K. C. Layne.
PHOTOS COURTESY OF:
K. C. LAYNE.

KIM SUMMERS

Kim started dancing when she was four. In 1959, she became a professional dancer at the age of sixteen, when she was hired as a chorus girl in her home town of Miami, Florida. She worked in several National and International production shows over a period of twenty-five years. She danced occasionally in shows at many of the major hotels in Las Vegas including, *Minsky's Follies* at the New Frontier, and *Thoroughly Modern Minsky* at the Thunderbird. Kim also worked with such performers as Sally Rand, comedienne Billie Bird, and comic Sid Fields, who was featured as the landlord on *The Abbott & Costello Show* on television. In-between production shows, she danced in burlesque theatres and supper clubs across the West coast and the Midwest, as well as the rest of the United States. As a solo act, Kim became proficient as a fan dancer, and in the 1970s, she performed "The Love Act," a dance routine with a male partner. When she changed partners, they became "The Summer Affair." In 1984, Kim Summers retired, but continued to work as a dance studio operator, choreographer for several musicals for two local Light Opera Companies, and has taught dance for many years. She also served as a dance director and choreographer for a performing dance company. Kim Summers has definitely aged gracefully into her later years.

LADY MIDNIGHT

Benita Kirkland was born into a show business family. Benny "Beans" Kirkland, a blackface vaudeville performer, was her grandfather. Her parents were Monkey Kirkland, a comedian and actor, and Josephine Field, a dancer and actress. Later, Kay Drew became her stepmother. There was no doubt that Benita would become a performer. As a baby, she made her first appearance on stage in her parents Tent-Show production of *Uncle Tom's Cabin*. However, her debut in burlesque happened at the age of twenty, when Monkey hired his daughter to perform in his nightclub, Collette's, in Phoenix, Arizona. Kay Drew taught the young dancer how to strip, yet still be a lady, and that it was not necessary to sleep with anyone to get to the top. She was taught that she just needed talent and experience.

Having a baby girl to care for, and after dancing for only a few weeks at the club, she needed to escape an abusive husband. Everyone at Collette's pitched in to help Benita flee to Los Angeles. Kay instructed her stepdaughter to go to the Follies Theatre as soon as she arrived. Monkey was well-known there, and she was sure the owner would help. Bob Biggs, the manager, said that if Benita could dance, she could join the chorus line until there was an opening for a stripper. Benita loved it, and Lillian Hunt seemed happy to have the talented young dancer in the chorus line. It was not more than a couple of weeks before one of the strippers hurt her knee and Benita replaced her in the show. When Biggs asked what her stage name would be, Benita remembered that a Greyhound bus had brought her to Los Angeles around midnight, so she said, "Midnight." Soon after, she changed her stage name to "Lady Midnight," and the name stuck.

For four consecutive years, Lady Midnight performed at the Follies as co-feature and lead talking woman. Later, she worked many Los Angeles area clubs before going back to the Follies as a feature. In 1964, in a much-publicized wedding in front of a large audience, she married comic Jimmy Mathews on the Follies Theatre stage. A few weeks later, they went on the road working the burlesque circuit in Pittsburgh, Baltimore, Akron, Dayton, and Cleveland. In Toledo, they worked for Rose La Rose.

Some of the dancers she worked with included Jennie Lee, Taffey O'Neil, Gay Dawn, Kay Drew, Caprice, Holly Parks, Patti Waggin, Tempest Storm, Valkyra, Betty Rowland, Jody Lawrence, Naja Karamuru, Georgia Holden, Electra, Nona Carver, Novita, Toni Baldwin, Coquette, Brandy Alexander, and Virginia "Ding-Dong" Bell. A few of the comics she performed alongside included Bobby Faye, Harry Clexx, Bozo Lord, Joey Faye, Sammy Price, and her father, Monkey Kirkland.

Midnight recalled, "I remember when Gypsy Rose Lee came backstage once and was a really nice, down-to-earth gal. She carried her trusty movie camera and asked if she could take pictures of me performing. Of course I said yes. So, she went out front and stood close to the runway, where she made a film of me dancing onstage."

Jess Mack represented Lady Midnight when she went on the road. Since there was a Diana Midnight already working back east,

Benita performed under the name "Jaguar." Then, after only a couple months of marriage, she and Jimmy parted ways. She hated working the circuit, and she loathed to flash, which was something she did not have to do in California. She decided to return home. Later, Gay Dawn mentioned that she also hated to flash. She got around it by covering herself with nude-colored moleskin, and brushing up the nap so it looked like hair.

When she was thirty, Lady Midnight decided to quit burlesque in order to spend more time with her daughter. However, she missed burlesque. In 1969, Benita was involved in a very serious car accident, which nearly took her life. Though she suffered from its effects, her attitude was, "It may have slowed me down, but it sure won't stop me!"

Lady Midnight.
PHOTOS COURTESY OF: LADY MIDNIGHT.

Jennie Lee.
Photo courtesy
of: Pat Flannery.

Taffey O'Neil.
Photo courtesy of:
Lady Midnight.

Holly Parks. Photo courtesy of: Holly Parks

LA SAVONA

La Savona originally came from Czechoslovakia, which is now the Czech Republic. She was an attraction in many European cities before moving to the United States. In Europe, dancing was recognized as a sensuous, ancient art form; the performance was most important, not how much clothing was worn. Her burlesque career began in New York City soon after her arrival. She worked as a special, added attraction on the same bill with Blaze Starr. When Blaze left, La Savona became the star of the show. She toured in theatres and clubs in the United States, Canada, and Europe. Some newspapers such as *Variety* reviewed her performance as "an interpretation of Sally Rand," but La Savona did not even know Sally Rand. La Savona's photos appeared on the cover of several magazines, as well as on two record albums. She also performed on radio, television, and in films. She is perhaps best known for her "Scheherazade Oriental" number, and she is most proud of the Honorary Membership bestowed upon her by the crew of the legendary atomic submarine *USS Seawolf*.

LaSavona. PHOTOS COURTESY OF: LASAVONA.

LaSavona.
Photos courtesy of: LaSavona.

LEE ANGEL

In 1956, Lee, also known as "Angel Robinson," began her burlesque career on the East coast in the Dave and Lucky Wilde's Review with the *World of Mirth*. She performed as lead dancer, straight woman, and barker. Due to her close friendship with rock and roll musician Little Richard, Lee was the only exotic dancer to headline shows on the Cetlin Circuit. In 1960, she was booked into the Blue Mirror Club in Washington, D.C., and she later performed at the Copa in Baltimore using the stage name, "Robin Lee." In 1963, Angel arrived ready to dance at the Coffer House in St. Thomas, Virgin Islands. However, her presence inspired the passing of a new law that would not allow her to perform her act in anything but a swimsuit. Lee went on to perform all over the world, becoming an international star. In 1977, she retired from burlesque.

Lee Angel.
PHOTOS COURTESY OF: LEE ANGEL.

Carnival days. Photo courtesy of: Lee Angel.

Group shot of Sepia Stars. Photo courtesy of: Lee Angel.

LEE FLOWERS

Lee began her career dancing in the chorus line at the Old Howard Theatre in Boston. Born in Avon Park, Florida, she moved to Boston after divorcing her husband in 1951. While working in the chorus line, she caught costumes off stage for Irma the Body, and the two women became good friends. When Lee decided to step out of the chorus line and become a strip, Irma sold her an old costume. Lee says she was scared to death when she walked out alone on that stage in 1952 for the first time.

She wrote, "I must explain, Rose La Rose was the big name when I started at the Old Howard. The Howard closed during the summers, and some of the chorus gals went to the Casino Theatre down the street and worked, since the same people owned both theatres. In those days, law officers were tough, and within a very short time, they closed down both theatres after a censor got into the theatres and caught Rose La Rose showing more than she should have. So that's when I went out and worked clubs. I had to mix in some clubs, but I never drank any real drinks."

Lee also once worked in Calumet City, just outside of Chicago. AGVA blackballed women within the union if they were caught working there. So when asked why she worked there, her reply was quite simple: "Because I wanted an adventure."

Performers Lee remembered working with included Rose La Rose, Georgia Sothern, Peaches, Irma the Body, Sally Keith, Petti Dane and Lou Ascol, Sheri Champagne, Tina Christine, and Anna Holland. Primarily, she worked for agent Jimmy Bell, but there were others. The one time that she performed in Florida, Lee was billed as "Honey Chile Lee" so family members would not know she was there. For decades, Lee never discussed her dancing career, but she remains quite proud to have been a part of old-time burlesque.

"The most wonderful, warm people I ever met worked in burlesque, but my folks never knew I was an exotic dancer. My family always thought I worked in a chorus line, but they thought it was in a stage show."

Sheri Champagne. Authors Collection.

Lee Flowers.
Photo courtesy of:
Lee Flowers.

LEE STUART

From 1947 to 1957, Lee was a house singer and straight man. Lee said, "I would have stayed in burlesque longer. I loved it while I was there, but the theatres were closing and there wasn't enough work to keep one busy."

Elaine, Lee's wife, was captain of the chorus line at the Gem Follies Theatre in Chicago when they first met. Once married, she went on the road with Lee and worked as a strip.

Lee wrote, "At twenty-one, I was very young to be a straight man. Most straight men were at least thirty years older than me. In order to fit in, I had to use makeup. I'd gray my temples with clown white and add a few lines to my face and from the front of the house I'd pass for fifty or more. Most of the comics were sixty or more at the time and a young punk shoving an old guy around wouldn't be funny to the audience."

"In 1954 after I married Elaine, she mentioned to me, 'Everyone thought that those old comics would eat you alive, because you were so young and they resented your youth.' But I hung in there and made it. I was young and eager to learn and out-lived the ones who considered me a threat."

"I'd stand in the wings and watch the better straight men work. It was an education for me. One of the tougher comics to please was Walter Brown. I was in Dayton when Milton Schuster called to tell me that I was to open at the Empress in Milwaukee the following week. When the guys on the show heard this, they laughed and told me that Walter was going to eat my lunch and that most straight men refused to work with him because he was so hard to please. Well, I needed the work and on the way to the job, I decided I'd tame the beast with kindness. When I first met Walter, backstage, I was humble and said, 'Mr. Brown, I'm your straight man for the next two weeks. Would you run over your scenes with me so I can learn what you want from me?' Walter was shocked that a straight man would be so interested in doing it right, because most brushed him off and made fun of him. Well, by the time the two weeks were up, Walter was calling Schuster, telling him what a great straight man I was and telling him to book me with him, anytime. I never worked with Walter again and it was a tough two weeks;

but I made a friend and next time I saw Schuster, he asked, 'What the hell did you do to Walter? You are the first straight man to please him in years.' All it took was a little understanding and humility, on my part. Word got around that if I could please Walter, I could please anyone; so I was welcome everywhere and my bookings increased."

Lee also stated, "I missed the hey-day of burlesque and got in on the very last few good years. But I left before the final curtain. I loved what I saw of it and was sorry to see it die, but die it did. There is a lot of published history that covers the so-called stars of the business; but very little about the supporting casts that really made up the nuts and bolts of the business. Most of that information died with the people who lived it."

Lee was very helpful in my efforts to preserve just some information regarding those supporting players. After retiring from burlesque, Lee and Elaine settled in Texas. "When Elaine and I left burlesque," he wrote, "We settled in Galveston and I began searching for a job. Let me tell you, experience in burlesque does not prepare one for work in the real world. After several tries, I finally found a job driving a truck for the Houston Chronicle circulation department. My job was to oversee the paperboys and deliver a paper route, myself. From that beginning, I stayed with them for thirty years and retired as head of the state circulation department. Had I stayed in burlesque, I'd have wound up like a lot of performers who fell on hard times."

"The paper route I delivered included the red light district in downtown Galveston and the town was wide open in those days. The first time I went to collect my route; I entered one of the houses to get my money from the madam who was a subscriber. I knocked on the door and told the lady I was there to collect for the paper. She ushered me into the parlor, where customers waited for an available lady. As I sat there waiting for the lady to return, I noticed a nice framed photo of Lotus DuBois on the wall. It had been taken from a girlie magazine and I suppose it was there to get the customers in the mood. I couldn't wait to get home and tell Elaine that her very close friend, Lotus DuBois' picture was hanging on the wall of a Galveston Whore House, which was something we laughed about for several days."

When Lee began performing in burlesque, few comics used scripts. When rehearsing scenes with the cast, they just winged it. However, he worked with comic Ray Kolb, who came from the old school. Kolb believed in working from a script, and some of them date back to the 1920s and 1930s. A few years after his retirement, he allowed Lee to make copies of this material. When I first asked about comedy bits, as the burlesque scenes were called, Lee sent me packet after packet of these scripts from which to make copies. All contained old-time burlesque scenes, three of which are included in this book.

Personally, I know of Ray Kolb only through materials donated to the Burlesque Historical Society from Lorraine Lee, Lee Stuart, the Watts Family, and Miss White Fury, but because of these items, we can now commit to memory a little information about this old-time burlesque comic.

In one letter that is in our collection, Kolb wrote, "I retired from the business in 1975, after sixty-four years of pounding the boards. My last engagement was at the Palace Theatre in Buffalo, New York. The show was cut down to six or seven people, and I just couldn't take it any longer. I had several offers after that—Ann Corio for one, but I turned it down."

Enclosed with his letter was a Thursday, January 15, 1981 newspaper article from the *Kentucky Enquirer*, which was written by Jack Hicks. The article stated that in 1981 at the age of eighty-eight, Ray recalled how show business was in his blood. When family members insisted his father become a priest, he climbed over the monastery wall and became a circus acrobat instead.

From his teens until 1975, Ray traveled on the burlesque circuit. Often working as a stage manager, as well as a comic, Kolb spoke of production companies with fifty or sixty people involved in a show. Once in Chicago, he worked a show where there were thirty-four chorus girls. He was proud to be a burlesque comic performing in humorous skits rather than stand-up comedy. Throughout his career, the bit Ray was most known for was "Bolivar the Elephant." It involved con men trying to sell an elephant to a near-sighted woman. Kolb was the back half of the elephant, and when interviewed for the article, he couldn't even remember how many times the gag was used.

His jokes were double-entendre, but never dirty. As Kolb explained in Hicks article, "First, radio and then television killed burlesque. In the early days, comedians couldn't use words like 'hell' or 'damn,' and the dancers were told how far they could go."

Kolb also told the reporter that his brother, who was also on the circuit, once hired a troupe of dancers in St. Joseph, Missouri, promising the woman who represented them that they would not appear in burlesque.

"That's what it was, of course, and the woman, whose daughters were among the dancers, filed suit when the show hit Louisville. Her daughters were Gypsy Rose Lee, who later became perhaps the greatest name in burlesque, and June Havoc, who went on to work in movies. Most of the theatres I've played have fallen prey to the wrecker's ball. Show business had its joys; however, it also had its sorrows."

All Ray Kolb, Lee Stuart, and others working in burlesque ever strived for was to entertain audiences and leave them laughing—and they succeeded. Unfortunately, on November 14th, 2007, we lost Lee Stuart.

Lee and Elaine Stuart at the Star Theatre in Portland, Oregon.
PHOTO COURTESY OF: LEE STUART.

Lee and Elaine Stuart at the Rivoli Theatre in Seattle, Washington.
PHOTO COURTESY OF: LEE STUART.

Lee Stuart.
PHOTO COURTESY OF: LEE STUART.

Elaine Stuart.
PHOTO COURTESY OF: LEE STUART.

Lotus DuBois.
PHOTO COURTESY OF: LEE STUART.

Comic Ray Kolb performing on stage at the National Theatre in Louisville, Kentucky.
PHOTO COURTESY OF: LEE STUART.

LIA LONDON

One of the younger members of The Golden Days of Burlesque Historical Society, Lia left home in Buffalo, New York at the age of fifteen to become a chorus girl. During the seventeen years she spent on the burlesque circuit, she performed all across the United States, as well as in Canada, Mexico, Australia, the Far East, and Guam. But she was not just a stripper. Billed as "California's Variety Girl," Lia was also a well-trained magician and voted Best Female Magician of 1976 by the Magic Dealers Association and the International Association of Magicians.

Lia said, "I was a performer who stripped but I was heavily into magic. I only got naked once, when I was doing my act for a very sophisticated men's club. Most of the guys were smoking grass, and I wasn't getting their attention. So I did my card-in-a-bottle trick while I was naked. At the clubs, it was the drunks who turned me off the most, but I loved traveling. I really got off on being on the road; it appealed to my spirit of adventure."

Lia irritated club owners when she openly objected to their instructions to hustle customers for drinks between her acts. She brought a creative vision to her work, which was never embarrassing or awkward, and was always entertaining. She often performed four separate acts each night, which included tap and belly dancing, along with card and sleight-of-hand tricks.

Lia had always loved the ocean. In 1970 while performing in Guam, she learned to scuba dive. In 1973, she and her husband sat in a Newport Beach restaurant discussing their future. Lia's dream was to set sail and explore new places. As a sailboat cut across the bay, Lia said, "That's what I want!" They worked diligently and separately for four years, and in 1978, they eventually saw their dream come true. Life changed for Lia, when she and her husband watched *Wet Dream*, their thirty-eight-foot sailboat, splash into the water after it was refurbished by the San Pedro Boat Works. They fished commercially in Alaska to gain the necessary experience to qualify her for a captain's license, which Lia received in 1982 from the United States Coast Guard. She was authorized to operate or navigate passenger carrying vessels.

For Lia, the sea became her home. She began a yacht charter business called Sail San Diego, with which she offered instructional sailing cruises, charters to Catalina and Mexico, whale-watching excursions, as well as customized bay cruises. In time, Lia moved to Hawaii. She continued offering sailboat excursions to Tahiti, as well as attaining her degree in engineering.

In late 2004, reluctantly and solely due to health reasons, Lia returned to living on land. She gave up her boat and her life on the water. In January 2005, Captain Lia, as she was affectionately called, passed away.

Lia London.
PHOTO COURTESY OF: LIA LONDON/BURLESQUE HISTORICAL SOCIETY.

Lia London's sailboat, "Wet Dream."
PHOTO COURTESY OF: LIA LONDON/BURLESQUE HISTORICAL SOCIETY.

Lia London.
PHOTO COURTESY OF:
LIA LONDON/BURLESQUE
HISTORICAL SOCIETY.

Lilli Marlene

In 1942, Sigrid Schroter was born in a small village surrounded by the Alpine Mountains in Sparwiesen, Germany. At a young age, she stood on a chair so she could be heard and began singing and reciting poetry at various family and community events. After growing up, Sigrid played the leads in her school productions. She continually dreamed of becoming an actress, but her parents pushed her into linguistics because they wanted her to become an interpreter.

Upon graduation, she spoke fluent English. Sigrid found work as a switchboard operator with the US Army Signal Division at Cook Barracks in Goeppingen, Germany. Often after work, she played the piano and sang at the Service Club with her American friends, and when one suggested that they start a band, she was asked to be their lead singer. Sigrid accepted immediately and began her new career as singer and dancer with The Dynamics. The five-piece band performed as an opening act for The Temptations, Lionel Hampton, The Four Aces, and other headliners from the United States. They toured together for many years, singing at army bases all across Germany. It was on one of these trips that she met her future husband. After marrying, the young couple moved to Milwaukee, Wisconsin, where Sigrid did some sportswear modeling work for Haertlein Graphics, her father-in-law's business.

One day while sunning herself by Lake Michigan, a local photographer for the *Milwaukee Journal* snapped Sigrid's photo and it was printed on the front page of the newspaper. A few days later, she was approached by Ray Auler, a Chicago agent, and asked if she would be interested in touring with a burlesque troop. After convincing her of the potential financial gain, she accepted. Sigrid was whisked off to Chicago to pose for publicity shots by star photographer Maurice Seymour. Then, she was outfitted with beaded gowns, extravagant headpieces, feather boas, g-strings, and rhinestone bikinis. The troop included five dancers, a male comedian, an emcee, and a stagehand. They rehearsed for weeks, and then they toured all over the United States and Germany. They played theatres and nightclubs until 1968, when Sigrid started her own show performing mostly in the Midwest and occasionally in Germany. Then in 1968, she was crowned Miss Stuttgart Germany.

Some of the routines for which she was famous included the Lilli Marlene song, "Underneath the Lamplight," which required the assistance of a male partner dressed as a World War Two sailor. Also she performed "The Rites of Spring" with fire, thunder, and smoke coming from a specialized smoke machine, while she wore a fabulous white costume. In that routine, the stage was set with black lights and a mirrored revolving strobe light. Lilli also shared the stage with thousands of bubbles from a bubble machine. She performed her final show in Chicago, after her agent passed away in 1973.

After hanging up her gowns Sigrid changed careers by attending Milwaukee Technical College, where she studied beauty and skin care. Upon graduation, she began her own business called The Mequon Hair Square. She worked with models, stage shows, local celebrities, and performers, and she did many before-and-after makeovers for magazine layouts. In 1983, she met her current husband, a Marquette University Tennis Coach, and they sold their business and moved to Florida.

Sigrid was not happy being retired, so she created an exceptionally upscale skin care salon called "Sigrid of Germany," while her husband runs a successful consulting business. After raising two sons and maintaining her own business, Sigrid has also been involved with writing children's books and novels, occasionally acting with a local theatre group, and singing in her church choir. When Florida hurricane seasons got to be too much to handle for the Midwestern family, they moved to South Carolina. Sigrid actively works with the Greenwood German Ladies Society, and she remains surrounded by loving family, friends, and her Dachshunds.

Lilli Marlene.
Photo courtesy of:
Lilli Marlene.

Lilli Marlene. PHOTO COURTESY OF: LILLI MARLENE.

LINDA DOLL

In 1949, Linda Doll began performing as a teenager at the Folly Theater in Kansas City, Missouri. She featured in clubs and theatres in twenty-eight states and Canada, working until 1969.

Linda told the following story regarding a performance of her infamous fire dance one evening. The house lights went out, and her tassels were already lit on fire and twirling to the beat of the band, when one came off and flew across the room in mid-air. Laughing, yet screaming, people ran for cover, but she never got her tassel back. Whoever found it kept it as a souvenir. No damage was done, and the Fire Department allowed Linda to keep her fire permit.

Upon retiring from burlesque, Linda, a member of the American Guild of Variety Artists, as well as the Screen Actors Guild, began performing bit parts and dancing as an extra in movies or television shows, most notably in *Viva Las Vegas* with her good friend, Elvis Presley. All totaled, she appeared in nearly sixty-five projects starring performers such as Gale Storm, Bob Hope, John Wayne, Jackie Gleason, Jimmy Stewart, Patricia Neal, James Garner, Gene Kelly, and most recently, the 1990 Julia Roberts film, *Pretty Woman*. Linda Doll also felt honored to have met Harry Truman, John F. Kennedy, Richard Nixon, and Ronald Reagan.

Linda Doll posing for the photographer.
PHOTO COURTESY OF: LINDA DOLL.

Linda Doll.
PHOTO COURTESY OF: LINDA DOLL.

Linda Doll's Memory Board.
PHOTO COURTESY OF: LINDA DOLL.

Linda Doll publicity post card.
PHOTO COURTESY OF: LINDA DOLL.

"Tulsa Glamour Queen," Linda Doll appearing in a 1958 Tulsa, Oklahoma, parade.
PHOTO COURTESY OF: LINDA DOLL.

Lilac, with large painted silver dots, Linda Dolls' 1953 car helped to advertise her performances at the York Club.
PHOTO COURTESY OF: LINDA DOLL.

LORRAINE LEE

Lorraine, a strong supportive member of The Golden Days of Burlesque Historical Society, was instrumental in helping preserve the history of comic Dick Richards, her late husband, but it was almost a struggle getting her to discuss her own career.

Lorraine wrote, "In late summer 1937, I took a note from my mother to the Joy Theatre in Houston, Texas. The note asked if they could use me as a chorus girl. I gave the note to "Red" St. Clair. I'd known "Red" for many years after we first met in Seminole, Oklahoma. "Red" was a "Blues" singer and did scenes."

"Seminole had three theatres—two with stage shows. One had Benny "Beans" Kirkland, Monkey's father, and Slats Taylor performing along with chorus girls, a straight man, and house singer. The State Theatre had comic Bozo St. Clair, Jack Arnold as the straight man and singer, "Red" St. Clair, and a chorus line of at least six girls, including the Cannon Sisters. The Cannon sisters taught my sister and me the Waltz Clog, after which we entered amateur night contests."

"The Joy had two movies, a news reel, comedy shorts, and four stage shows a day. Matinee admissions were only 10¢, and shows at night were only 25¢, seven days a week. The stage show changed three times a week, running from Sunday to Monday, Tuesday through Thursday, and then Friday, Saturday, and a "Midnight Rumble." The Rumble had the same dance routines and specialty numbers as Sunday and Monday, but also included racy bits, pose numbers, a strip, an opening number with all the girls and the singer, comics, and singers. The finale lasted two to four minutes."

"From Tuesday through Thursday, we did a "book show," where we performed shorter versions of a play or Broadway show. In one show, I was the wife from *The Taming of the Shrew* and got to snap a whip after the comic. Rehearsals were held on Monday, Thursday and Friday, at 11:15pm, 1:30am, and 2:00am."

The Joy Theatre hired me, but I only worked in the opening number. The producer put on a newsboy routine, and then we all waltz-clogged to "East Side, West Side." I spent all my time watching the other dancers. I got no salary. The first week, the boss just bought me an ice cream cone every night. The second week, I received 50¢ cents, and then I was gradually increased to $10 per week by the end of ten months. The rest of the chorus was making $12; however, they had been in the business for years."

"Every chorus girl had to do a strip on Saturday night. We took turns about every six weeks and received an extra $1.50 in our envelope for the week. When I did my first strip, girls were in the wings on both sides of the stage, telling me what to take off and when to do it."

"The costumes were generally a hat or headpiece, long gloves, jacket, dress, a solid bra, a net bra with big pasties underneath, a fringed skirt, a sheer chiffon panel, and net pants to the waist with a large pink patch covering us front and back. The audience screamed and stomped their feet, always wanting more."

"In the beginning, I worked quite a few theatres around Dallas, Houston, San Antonio, New Orleans, and Knoxville. When I finally went on the burlesque circuit, I worked theatres all across the United States. Later, I worked clubs. I was almost always the first strip after the opening, because I needed to get ready to do the comedy scenes. I did a parade strip—no bumps and grinds—it was an interesting way of losing my clothes. I never showed much, since my long hair covered my breasts."

"If a comic was married or involved with a stripper, as a rule, she did his scenes so that he didn't have to rehearse a new woman every week. When a comic found someone that could remember lines and was dependable, he usually used her in all his scenes."

"One of my favorite strips was where I wore a three-piece outfit consisting of a long robe, jacket, skirt with beaded fringe, and a beaded bra. I performed to one chorus of "Sleepy Time Gal," one chorus of "I'll See You in My Dreams," and one chorus of "Good Night Sweetheart." I also did a fan dance number in a simple white gown, rhinestone pants, and a net bra with large feather fans. I danced to three choruses of "Jealousy.""

"I have no idea when I performed my last strip. I just remember seeing a few things on stage that I didn't care for, so I just stuck to talking in scenes. In 1987, I did my last scene in Miami Beach in a show at a hotel with my husband, Dick Richards."

Lorraine Lee. PHOTO COURTESY OF: LORRAINE LEE.

MARA GAYE

Mara Gaye was billed as "Exotic Surprise" and "The Lady of Fashion." She began performing in theatre productions at a very young age, before winning the title of Miss Dallas 1936. In the late 1930s, she became a Radio City Music Hall Rockette and danced in the line for five years. She had a brief career appearing in films such as *The Mexican Hayride, My Dear Public,* and *The Devil on Horseback* with Ann Miller. Mara also danced in Billy Rose's Casa Manana Show and at the Clover Club in Miami.

In the early 1940s, she began her career in burlesque. She headlined in theatres and clubs across the United States, including Minsky's Empire Burlesque, the Hudson Theatre, Club Samoa, and the Willows. Mara also appeared in the *Paris Spice* edition of *Michael Rose Capers* at the Holiday Theatre on Broadway. Not only did she publish her own catalog of bizarre and exotic costumes, but her photos also appeared in many major publications. Friends and co-workers from burlesque included Georgia Sothern, Peaches, Lili St Cyr, and Sally Rand. In July of 2005, Mara Gaye passed away.

Mara Gaye. PHOTO COURTESY OF: MARA GAYE & THE SIEGFRIED FAMILY.

Meet Mara Gaye Flyer.
PHOTO COURTESY OF: MARA GAYE & THE
SIEGFRIED FAMILY.

Mara Gaye publicity post card.
PHOTO COURTESY OF: MARA GAYE
& THE SIEGFRIED FAMILY.

Mara Gaye publicity post card.
PHOTO COURTESY OF: MARA
GAYE & THE SIEGFRIED FAMILY.

Mara Gaye.
PHOTO COURTESY OF: MARA GAYE & THE
SIEGFRIED FAMILY.

Front of Club Samoa, featuring Mara Gaye.
PHOTO COURTESY OF: MARA GAYE & THE
SIEGFRIED FAMILY.

Mara Gaye standing in the archway of the Troc Theatre in Philadelphia.
PHOTO COURTESY OF: MARA
GAYE & THE SIEGFRIED FAMILY.

Holiday Theatre Marquee featuring Mara Gaye.
PHOTO COURTESY OF: MARA GAYE & THE SIEGFRIED FAMILY.

MARG C

Known as "The Irish Mist," Marg worked clubs and theatres across the Eastern Seaboard, west into Ohio and Minnesota, and into Canada. Paul Jordan and John Sullivan were her primary agents in Boston. Recently retired from working in the health care field, Marg has donated much of her time volunteering in the New Orleans area. Some of her costumes have been donated to the Bates Museum in Hinkley, Maine and Bates College in Lewiston, Maine. The rest, some made by Hedi Jo Starr, will be donated to the University of Ottawa, from which she received her B.A. Degree.

Marg C.
PHOTOS COURTESY OF:
MARG C.

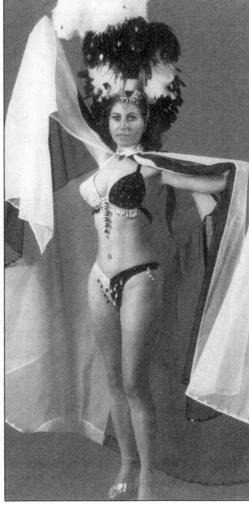

MARILYN MARZETTE

Marzette was known as "Marilyn the Calendar Girl." Little is known about Marilyn's career, just that she worked in burlesque theatres and clubs across the United States from the 1950s and beyond. I found Marilyn quite by accident when I went for a haircut in Las Vegas. We talked about burlesque, and she loaned me one of her albums to copy. After returning it, I never saw her again. We briefly corresponded through the mail, but her newsletters were returned.

Marilyn Marzette, "The Calendar Girl."
PHOTO COURTESY OF: MARILYN MARZETTE.

Marinka

Also known as "Melanie Hunter," Marinka danced as a feature on the burlesque circuit in theatres and nightclubs from the 1960s, including the Ann Corio show, *This Was Burlesque*, and the world-famous Crazy Horse Nightclub and Casino. She is very proud of the guidance and training she received from Rose La Rose. Marinka also appeared in films and performed in legitimate theatre productions, including, *All That Jazz*. She performed all over the United States, as well as Canada, Mexico, Lebanon, and Europe, including a special performance for the Shah of Iran. Marinka is always willing to perform whenever an audience wants to see a true, old-time burlesque routine.

Marinka.
Photos courtesy
of: Marinka.

Marvan

Born Violet Capellaro, she was the daughter of Dominic Capellaro, one-time owner of the National Wine Company in Washington State. She began studying dance at the age of twelve, and soon became a chorus girl at the State Theatre in Seattle, which was later renamed the Rivoli Theatre. Her initial career was brief. When her mother found out, she forced her young daughter off the stage. In 1939, working in a place of that sort was considered a sin. Upon graduating from Franklin High School, Violet attended the University of Washington and studied drama. She loved to dance, so in 1941, she headed to San Francisco. Violet not only studied at the San Francisco Opera Ballet, but she also danced at John's Rendezvous. She studied modernistic dance, as well as tumbling and acrobatic dance. In 1942, Violet headed back to Seattle and did her part for the war effort by working at the Boeing plant as a riveter. In 1943, she went back to California and danced in San Diego. Up until then, she had stuck to legitimate dancing, but she changed directions.

"Marvan said, "I saw those burlesque girls doing a whole lot less work, making a whole lot more money, and not exposing themselves anymore than I was, so I decided to become more commercial."

In 1945, Marvan headed to Boston where she worked as a showgirl in the famous Latin Quarter shows. In 1946, she went back to San Francisco, and then in 1949 to 1950, she worked in Los Angeles at the Burbank Theatre. She always preferred working in the theatres and clubs on the West coast. In 1951, after spending some time traveling with family members, she opened at the Rivoli Theatre in Seattle and remained there for the rest of her career in burlesque.

Marvan wrote, "After working at the Rivoli in the early 1950s, I married the owner. So I controlled backstage and Al controlled things up front. We had some wonderful people work for us including Gay Dawn, Jennie Lee, and most of Lillian Hunts' prodigies. It was a wonderful time in our life. We had so many good people around us. I trained quite a few girls while I was there too, and it was great fun."

Marvan and Al have long since retired. They spent considerable time traveling and enjoying the company of old friends until Marvan passed away on March 7th, 2008.

Rivoli Theatre, Seattle, Washington. PHOTO COURTESY OF: LEE STUART.

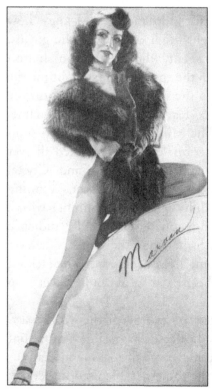

Marvan.
PHOTOS COURTESY OF: LEE STUART.

MARY ROONEY

Born in Brooklyn, New York, Mary was placed in an orphanage at the age of three after her parents separated. The orphanage was also part of a convent, and at one point, Mary considered becoming a nun, but she had a change of heart. She left the orphanage at age sixteen, dreaming only about becoming a movie star. She answered a newspaper ad to work as a waitress in a beautiful nightclub in New York City. She lied about her age, and was then hired by the glamorous owner, Lonnie Young. Lonnie, a former exotic dancer, who performed with snakes, said to Mary, "You have a beautiful body. Why don't you use it, and don't abuse it?" When Mary asked what she meant, Lonnie led her to one of many large wardrobe closets filling her home. It overflowed with beautiful gowns. Selecting one, she handed it to Mary and instructed her to put the gown on. Switching on the record player, Lonnie said, "Now get out of it."

Mary wrote, "My passion is music and dancing, so I knew how to move to the music. Lonnie taught me how to work the gowns. Then she took me to her theatrical agent, who used to book her on shows years ago, and he hired me on the spot. Lonnie taught me the game and I played it all the way to the top. I first traveled on the circuits for forty weeks a year as a co-feature. I used my own name, Mary Rooney, with the billing, "The Million Dollar Baby." I soon became the headliner and star attraction, and I was featured all over the country. I also danced under the names "Chris Snow" and "Crystal La-Vegas, The Girl with the Golden Nuggets and the Winning Numbers." Working as Crystal, I did a production number with a 300-pound prop roulette table and revolving wheel. The audience was invited on stage, and one by one, they spun the wheel. Wherever the wheel stopped, that's the clothing item I removed. The jackpot was the g-string, but I had the wheel fixed so it would never stop there—but the guys sure did try."

Mary worked all over the United States, except the West coast. She also worked in Canada and had offers to work in London, but she turned them down due to the high cost of making alterations for European electrical current in the roulette table used in her act. She also turned down work in Spain due to a clause in the contract that stated they could cancel her contract any time they did not like her act. Mary's only request was that they put her money in escrow. They refused, so she did not accept the contract.

"I was not worried about my act, because I always worked with class, but I was worried about working and not being paid, or being stranded in Europe. Lou Walters also offered me work in Paris. Lou owned the world-famous Latin Quarter Club in New York City, and he also owned a club in Paris called The Crazy Horse. This was another job I turned down because I was not being hired as an exotic dancer. I was to sit and pose on a wooden carousel horse that circled the bar. Several other girls seated on wooden horses that connected to this carousel were posing. I really didn't think that job was very artistic, or that the pay made it worthwhile. The thought of going to Paris was very exciting, but I also thought I'd get dizzy riding a carousel for eight hours each night, so I said 'thank you, but no thank you.'"

Mary was proud of several letters she wrote and magazines published in defense of old-time burlesque and the art of exotic dancers. She also took great pride in a project she began working on in 1972, but was unable to complete due to circumstances beyond her control.

Mary wrote, "I wrote Count Basie, asking him to produce an LP of his music for us exotic dancers. He responded immediately, and he and his manager met me for dinner where we all agreed this was a worthwhile project. Terms were discussed and our work had already begun when I learned the Count had become seriously ill. Needless to say, the project was postponed and I was devastated when he died before the album could be completed."

In 1957, Mary began dancing at age sixteen, and to this very day she still loves to dance. She said, "I can dance up a storm, even on a dance floor packed with teenagers. I just have music and rhythm in my bones."

Victory Theatre marquee advertising "The Million Dollar Baby," Mary Rooney.
Photo courtesy of: Mary Rooney.

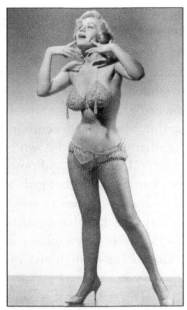

Mary Rooney.
PHOTOS COURTESY OF: MARY ROONEY.

Mary Rooney, performing at the Victory Theatre in Toronto, Canada, 1967. Robert Suzuki, Photographer.
PHOTO COURTESY OF: MARY ROONEY.

Crystal La-Vegas.
PHOTO COURTESY OF: MARY ROONEY.

Gayety Burlesk newspaper ad.
PHOTO COURTESY OF: MARY ROONEY.

MIMI REED AND THAREEN AURORAA

Around 1931, Mimi Reed began working in burlesque as a specialty dancer and talking woman. She worked with some of the greatest burlesque comics and performers of her day, including Rags Ragland, Hank Henry, Red Buttons, Phil Silvers, Joe De Rita, Joey Faye, Bobby Morris, Robert Alda, and Abbott & Costello. Featured strippers she knew and worked with included Gypsy Rose Lee, Ann Corio, and Margie Hart. Mimi retired from the burlesque stages by 1947, after which she partnered with former opera singer Thareen Auroraa. They traveled and performed together for years in supper clubs and nightclubs as Mimi Reed and Thareen Auroraa, "Nutty But Nice." Their billing was perfect. In March 2006, Thareen passed away. Nine months later, Mimi died one month after her ninety-seventh birthday. Mimi and Thareen were two of the nicest women you could ever hope to meet.

LEFT TO RIGHT: **Thareen Auroraa and Mimi Reed.**
PHOTO COURTESY OF: MIMI REED/BURLESQUE HISTORICAL SOCIETY.

Mimi Reed.
PHOTOS COURTESY OF: BURLESQUE HISTORICAL SOCIETY.

MISS WHITE FURY

This fan favorite, also known as "Patti Kelly," usually worked under the name "Miss White Fury and her Twin 44's." Her parents, Rusty and Dusty Farnham, worked in vaudeville and early radio. From 1953 to 1983, "Miss White Fury" performed all over the country in theatres and clubs. Coralie Jr. was her agent, and tassel twirling was her specialty.

MITZI

In 1917, Mitzi was born in Chicago to dancers Mickey and Elsie McGarry. Mitzi spent her childhood on the vaudeville circuit. She and I met several times over the years, with our talks usually revolving around her career. She told me, "By the age of three, I was already starring in my own act, "Baby Darling," and singing, "Ma, He's Making Eyes at Me!" to the drummer. He'd always act like he was shy which made people laugh. I'd also perform a little dance imitating my mom, finish with the splits, and then I'd take my bow. When it was time for me to get my schooling, I was sent to Toledo, Ohio, to stay with relatives, but during the summer months, I'd go on the road with my folks. I loved it and can't think of anything that was more fun to do, especially for a child."

In the early 1930s, the McGarry's opened a dance studio in Toledo. In 1938, Mickey passed away from tuberculosis. Soon after, Elsie went to live with Mitzi's best friend, dancer Val Valentine's mother. Elsie eventually moved in with Mitzi, and passed away in the late 1970s while living in Florida. Mitzi taught dance lessons at her parent's studio, in addition to dancing at a few local clubs and area hospitals. Once prohibition had been repealed, small nightclubs sprang up or reopened everywhere, so there was plenty of work for the young dancer.

Mitzi said, "When Sally Rand hit the big time with her fan number, the whole country went crazy. I even got some fans, so my mother made me a costume and we worked up a routine. I performed locally as a fan dancer for a long time. After a while though, exotic dancers all became the rage. This was during the end of the 1930s or so. I was still a kid tap-dancing in nightclubs, but agents and audiences all wanted exotics, so I decided to go into burlesque, where I had the opportunity of becoming a features star. I went to the Roxy

Theatre in Cleveland to see a burlesque show, and it was so professional with good acts, a chorus line, costumes, and a great orchestra."

Impressed, Mitzi signed on with Milton Schuster in Chicago, the best-known agent for the western circuit. He sent her to Detroit, where after one week, she co-featured. Then, she went to perform in Youngstown, Ohio, as the feature. Mitzi was popular with audiences everywhere, and she loved to dance—something that always shined through in her performances. For nearly four years, she regularly played the Rialto Theatre in Chicago for producer Paul Morokoff, who continually gave her fourteen-week contracts.

The late Peter "Sonny" Thomas recalled, "Mitzi had a very strong personality, which is one reason why the Rialto Theatre in Chicago featured her for long runs. She drew repeat business. She seemed to literally 'live' at the Rialto. Mitzi came in on a fourteen-week contract, and then went on the road. Before we new it, she was back at the Rialto."

Some of Mitzi's routines included "Dance of the Lovers," a half-and-half act, a wedding number, and "Dance of the Hands." She also twirled tassels to the music of "I Wish I could Shimmy like My Sister Kate." Mitzi proudly told me once, "I didn't do the naughty stuff, but I wasn't a weak act, talent-wise, either."

Like many dancers, Mitzi loved carnival life. She was featured twice on Royal, three times for Jack Norman on Strates, and several times for Raynell Golden on the Cetlin and Wilson Shows. She was married to Roland Parker for twenty years and the couple sometimes ran their own girl shows. Mitzi performed into her eighties at nursing homes, Veterans' Hospitals, and Exotic World. In early 2004, she passed away in Southern California.

Mitzi.
PHOTO COURTESY OF: VAL VALENTINE.

Mitzi.
PHOTO COURTESY OF: VAL VALENTINE.

MITZI DOERRE

Billed as "The Cuban Cutie" and "The I Don't Care Girl," Mitzi was later known in her career as "Lani Love." In 1945, she began her burlesque career at the age of twenty-two, in Panama. She worked all over the United States, including Hawaii. In 1954, she also worked in Canada, Japan, Europe, Germany, and all across the Orient. Mitzi preferred working in clubs, and she never danced totally nude. Towards the end of her career, she performed in Hawaii and enjoyed it so much that she stayed, working on the television show, *Hawaii 5-0.*

Mitzi Doerre, also known as Lani Love.
PHOTO COURTESY OF: MITZI DOERRE.

Mitzi Doerre.
PHOTO COURTESY OF: MITZI DOERRE.

MONA VAUGHN

In 1909, Carmella "Mona" Vaughn was born in St. Louis, Missouri. In 1927 when her parents moved to Washington State, Mona knew if she wanted to stay in the Midwest, she needed to find a job. The eighteen-year-old had no high school degree, but she found her destiny once she opened the newspaper. Mona spotted an ad that stated, "Wanted: Girls to Work Stock. Apply Garrick Theatre." Mona wandered into the theatre, and even though she had no formal training in dance, she secured a job as a chorus line dancer. This launched a thirty-five-year career in burlesque that kept her on stage working in theatres, clubs, stag shows, and girl shows in carnivals. Mona was an original member of The Golden Days of Burlesque Historical Society. She passed away in the spring of 2001.

Mona Vaughn, from the 1930s.
PHOTO COURTESY OF: MONA VAUGHN/BURLESQUE HISTORICAL SOCIETY.

Mona Vaughn.
PHOTO COURTESY OF:
MONA VAUGHN/BURLESQUE
HISTORICAL SOCIETY.

Norma Jean Watts

Norma Jean began her career in the chorus line at the Mayfair Theatre in Dayton, Ohio. She was fifteen and lied about her age to get the job. Norma Jean helped design and sew costumes for the burlesque shows in which she appeared. She also used to make false eyelashes for the other dancers with whom she worked. Buying the thinnest thread she could find, she could cut a single long human hair from a girl, which she then cut into single short pieces. These shorter hairs were glued onto individual pieces of thread and adhered to a base attached to the eyelids.

Norma Jean said, "It took many hours to make a set, which would last about two weeks before falling apart." At the age of seventeen, she married comic Art Watts. He thought she was twenty-four. After their marriage, Norma Jean continued to dance in chorus lines and performed all across the country as a talking woman in scenes with her husband.

When I asked people about Norma Jean, I was told she was quiet and rarely had much to say. Her family agreed, stating, "Yes, she was quiet, but she was extremely quick-witted and funny. Because Art and Norma Jean were always attached at the hip and went everywhere together, I understand why she didn't talk much. Later in life after Art died, it was extremely hard to get her to talk about her days in burlesque. Surprisingly, she was a very modest and private woman."

Val Valentine wrote, "Norma Jean and Art Watts were two of my dearest friends. We worked together in many theatres, and for several years during the summer months in the Big Girl Shows that were produced by Gene Vaughn on the James E. Strates Carnival Show. Norma was a young chorus girl in Dayton, Ohio. She and Art met there and got married. They were a true team. He was a funny comic, and she was a great talking woman. They were a true team in life, as well. For years, they had a ranch in Arkansas, and later, they opened a restaurant called Simple Simon's Restaurant. My son loved them both, and he can do Art's bits. He's even taught his four-year-old daughter some of them."

Art worked with Bob Hope and Jack Benny, and he was actor Robert Mitchum's favorite comic. Mitchum frequently attended burlesque shows and was often seen talking to Art backstage after a show ended for the evening. Norma said, "Arthur was good; he just never made the transition to the big time."

In 1974, while working the Strates Show at the North Carolina State Fair, the Raleigh, North Carolina *News and Observer* carried a story by Dan Loh Wasser that included the following comments by Art Watts:

"I don't think there are ten real burlesque comics left around. When I broke into burlesque, a show consisted of eighteen to twenty chorus girls alone and several different types of comics, but no strippers. This is the last place you can find real burlesque. Strates has the last of the traveling shows. Our jokes are spicy, modern, risqué, and double-entendre. Everything has a double meaning. Along with the tent shows, the old burlesque houses that were once found in every large city have for the most part disappeared. The biggest problem is finding entertainers. A young guy today doesn't want to take the time to learn this business. A carnival is like a small town, or a small community. You make a lot of good friends. It's the only real gypsy life left, and that's speaking as an old gypsy."

While working in Panama, Art created one of his better known bits, which lived or died on its double meanings. He and Norma Jean often performed the routine. They came out on stage where he told her he had figured out a commercial that consisted of names and slogans of all cigarettes, which he had blended in his own unique way: "One Kool morning, Miss Pall Mall took a stroll down Chesterfield Lane in Salem where she met Philip Morris, who took her to the Raleigh hotel in Winston. They got in that Old Gold bed. He slipped his King Size L&M in her old Zip Top Box. Man, he was in Marlboro country and was having a Lark because he was a Marvel with his Silky One Millimeter Longer. Now, after nine months, if she doesn't look like a Camel, baby, it's got to be a Lucky Strike. But she's not worried—she made him use a Filter Tip. They said it couldn't be done; but it's What's Up Front That Counts."

Art stated in one article, "We can't use the old vaudeville stuff any more because it would just be too corny. You always have to come up with new material."

Art knew about vaudeville because he was kicking around theatres and back stages since he ran away to join a medicine show in the early 1920s. He went back to the days when burlesque did not mean a strip show.

He stated in a 1975 interview, "When I was working during the depression, we were the poor man's opera. It was a clean show and the comic was the star. We had as many as twenty-five to thirty people on stage at one time during the show."

Art maintained that people had the wrong idea about show people, especially burlesque performers. He went on to say, "The strippers are all married. The people in the show travel together, see each other in the vacation months, and they are all friends."

In the old days, Art played a variety of comic styles, including tramps, eccentrics, and his specialty black-face. Art also said, "Of course, we can't do that anymore, but people used to love it. When we were on stage in black face, we weren't allowed to touch the white women. That's how far it went, but we didn't ridicule anybody."

Art played on the fringes of the big time, appearing with comics who later became stars. Art went on to state, "You have to stay on the borderline; everything has a double meaning. Forrest Tucker, best known for his role on *F-Troop*, used to be my straight man. Now, the foil of my jokes is my wife, Norma Jean. She feeds me the lines; I crunch on them for awhile, as I would Saltines, and then I spit them out in the form of Ritz Crackers. I always have a theme, but I like to ad lib and let it drift, and she's great for that. I never made the big time; I never was a star. It used to be the big thing was to play the Palace in New York. I never made it; maybe I wasn't good enough."

In 1988, Art Watts died at the age of eighty. On June 4, 2008, Norma Jean died.

Art and Norma Jean Watts being interviewed before working a carnival show.
Photo courtesy of: Norma Jean & Art Watts Family/Burlesque Historical Society.

Norma Jean Watts.
PHOTO COURTESY OF: NORMA JEAN &
ART WATTS FAMILY/BURLESQUE

**Norma Jean (far left) in a 1958
chorus line. Can anyone help the
BHS identify the rest of these
lovely ladies?**
PHOTO COURTESY OF: NORMA JEAN &
ART WATTS FAMILY/BURLESQUE
HISTORICAL SOCIETY.

**Norma Jean working a scene on
stage; she's the performer facing
the camera.**
PHOTO COURTESY OF: NORMA JEAN
& ART WATTS FAMILY/BURLESQUE
HISTORICAL SOCIETY.

Norma Jean Watts.
PHOTO COURTESY OF: NORMA JEAN
& ART WATTS FAMILY/BURLESQUE
HISTORICAL SOCIETY.

A young Art Watts.
PHOTO COURTESY OF: NORMA JEAN & ART WATTS
FAMILY/BURLESQUE HISTORICAL SOCIETY.

Art Watts.
PHOTO COURTESY OF:
NORMA JEAN & ART WATTS
FAMILY/BURLESQUE
HISTORICAL SOCIETY.

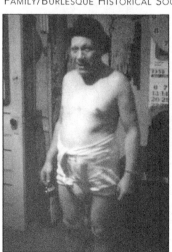

Art Watts "posing" backstage.
PHOTO COURTESY OF: NORMA
JEAN & ART WATTS FAMILY/
BURLESQUE HISTORICAL SOCIETY.

**Art Watts (center) on stage
with two other "characters"
performing a bit.**
PHOTO COURTESY OF: NORMA JEAN &
ART WATTS FAMILY/BURLESQUE
HISTORICAL SOCIETY.

Group shot backstage. Norma Jean Watts, Ava Leigh, Buddy O'Day and Art Watts; back row left to right. The couple in front is unknown; and the BHS needs your help identifying them.
PHOTO COURTESY OF: NORMA JEAN & ART WATTS FAMILY/BURLESQUE HISTORICAL SOCIETY.

Art and Norma Jean Watts smiling for the camera at home.
PHOTO COURTESY OF: NORMA JEAN & ART WATTS FAMILY/BURLESQUE HISTORICAL SOCIETY.

Art and Norma Jean Watts backstage.
PHOTO COURTESY OF: NORMA JEAN & ART WATTS FAMILY/BURLESQUE HISTORICAL SOCIETY.

Ray Kolb and Art Watts on stage.
PHOTO COURTESY OF: NORMA JEAN &
ART WATTS FAMILY/BURLESQUE
HISTORICAL SOCIETY.

Val Valentine.
PHOTO COURTESY OF: NORMA JEAN & ART WATTS FAMILY/ BURLESQUE HISTORICAL SOCIETY.

Lee Clifford and Art Watts working a bit.
PHOTO COURTESY OF: NORMA JEAN & ART WATTS FAMILY/BURLESQUE HISTORICAL SOCIETY.

Forrest Tucker.
PHOTO COURTESY OF: NORMA JEAN & ART WATTS FAMILY/ BURLESQUE HISTORICAL SOCIETY.

Ray Kolb, Art Watts, and Norma Jean Watts working together on stage.
PHOTO COURTESY OF: NORMA JEAN & ART WATTS FAMILY/BURLESQUE HISTORICAL SOCIETY.

Art and Norma Jean Watts performing a kissing booth scene.
PHOTO COURTESY OF: NORMA JEAN & ART WATTS FAMILY/BURLESQUE
HISTORICAL SOCIETY.

NOVITA

Novita performed in clubs as a child. In 1954, she began working in burlesque at the Follies Theatre in Los Angeles, where she was captain of the chorus line and performed tap, ballet, interpretive dance, and acrobatics. She also worked as a talking woman, performing in burlesque skits with comics such as Harry Clexx, Slats Taylor, Harry Savoy, Artie Lloyd, Bozo Lord, and Little Jack Little. When Novita tired of traveling, she developed a strip routine that allowed her to stay close to home and spend more time with her son. Working clubs and theatres, she was often the featured dancer in *The Lenny Bruce All Girl Revue*, opening the show with a tap dance routine.

In 1955, Jennie Lee, Novita, and seven other dancers formed the Exotic Dancers League (EDL). Those initially involved in the EDL included Jennie Lee, President and Founder, Novita, Vice-President, Rusty Lane, Betty Rowland, Virginia Valentine, Daurene Dare, Denise Dunbar, Peggy Stuart, and "Champagne." Absentee members included Pat Flannery, Doreen Gray, Caprice, and Misty Aires.

In 1957, Novita retired from burlesque, but remained an active member of EDL. Today, working under her real name, Rosie Mitchell is a professional artist with numerous paintings and sculptures in corporate and private collections. She's also currently writing her autobiography.

Rusty Lane.
PHOTO COURTESY OF: BURLESQUE
HISTORICAL SOCIETY.

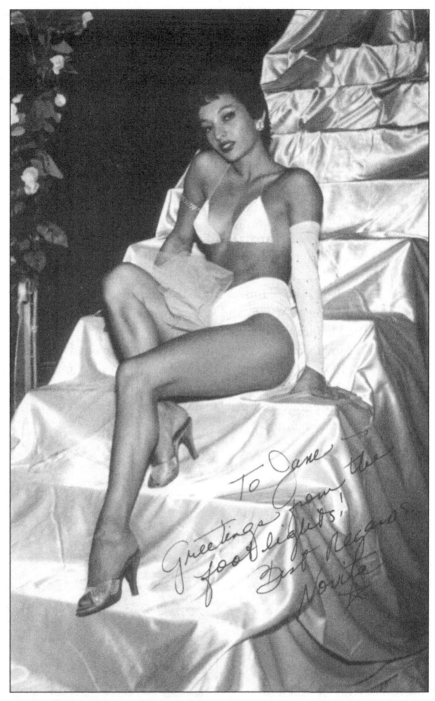

Novita. AUTHORS COLLECTION.

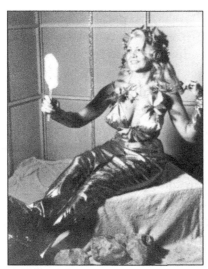

Jennie Lee.
Photo courtesy of: Pat Flannery.

Rusty Lane.
Photo courtesy of: Rusty Lane.

Doreen Gray.
Photo courtesy of:
Pat Flannery.

Caprice.
Photo courtesy of: Teri Starr.

PAT ELLIOTT

After studying dance in New York City, Pat performed in theatres, clubs, and in Las Vegas production shows from 1963 to 1967. She married burlesque producer, Harold Minsky. After their marriage, Pat worked behind the scenes learning the business end of producing the Minsky shows. In 1977 after Harold's death, Pat went on to co-produce two shows under the Minsky banner. Over the years, she remained active with charities and produced her own photography show. Pat continued to dance on occasion, and did some theatre and modeling, as well. She also produced glass art and was featured in the book, *Neon Queens*, by Gale Baker. After donating a large collection of burlesque related material to The Golden Days of Burlesque Historical Society, Pat Elliott Minsky died from cancer in November 2004.

Pat Elliott.
PHOTO COURTESY OF:
PAT ELLIOTT
MINSKY/BURLESQUE
HISTORICAL SOCIETY.

Pat Elliott.
PHOTO COURTESY OF: PAT ELLIOTT MINSKY/BURLESQUE HISTORICAL SOCIETY.

Pat Elliott.
PHOTO COURTESY OF: PAT ELLIOTT MINSKY/BURLESQUE HISTORICAL SOCIETY.

Pat Elliott Minsky and the World Famous Burlesque Thoroughly Modern Minsky Marquee, Las Vegas.
PHOTO COURTESY OF: PAT ELLIOTT MINSKY/BURLESQUE HISTORICAL SOCIETY.

PAT FLANNERY

Pat grew up surrounded by music. Her mother had been a performer in vaudeville and nightclubs. When vaudeville shows were closing down, she began playing piano in Honkytonks in San Francisco. Pat loved to dance, and she began her professional dancing career in chorus lines at the age of sixteen. After World War Two, she went to Los Angeles and found work in the movie industry. There was plenty of work to be had at MGM and Paramount, and Pat worked as an extra in many of the big-name musicals, including *Meet Me in St. Louis*. In the early 1950s, Pat began dancing in nightclubs and burlesque, performing as a satirical dancer, singer, and talking woman primarily on the West coast and in Alaska. Her favorite burlesque comics included "Beetle Puss" Lewis and Joe De Rita.

Due to her vast experience dealing with friends' horses, Pat also worked for a television studio teaching people how to mount and dismount, as well as how to be gentle and not spook the animals. Some of the shows she worked on included *Bonanza, Rawhide,* and *Gunsmoke*. Because of her love for horses she opened a dude ranch in San Bernardino, California. She had thirty-seven horses she saddled up each morning. The ranch also included a very popular restaurant. In 1960, Pat Flannery fully retired from burlesque, married, moved to the Midwest, raised three kids, and continues to love all types of animals.

Pat Flannery.
PHOTO COURTESY OF: PAT
FLANNERY.

Pat Flannery.
PHOTO COURTESY OF: PAT
FLANNERY.

Pat Flannery.
PHOTO COURTESY OF: PAT FLANNERY.

Patty O'Farrell

Patty was born and raised in California. As a child, she was enrolled in tap and ballet lessons. She thoroughly enjoyed dancing, and always performed what the music told her to do.

After marrying, she moved to the St. Louis, Missouri area and worked as a supervisor for the telephone company, where she first heard of agent Mike Riaff. Contacting Riaff, she expressed her interest in dancing. Soon after introductions were made, exotic dancer Dottie Carroll began showing Patty the ropes, which included helping develop routines, as well as making her first three costumes that cost around $100 each. Dottie was the feature at the Star Dust Night Club in St. Louis, and she helped arrange Patty's first, nervous appearance at the club. In the late 1950s, Riaff booked newcomers Patty O'Farrell and Julie Adorn (passed away in July 2006) into the Louisville, Kentucky burlesque theatre. Patty and Julie rode the train down together from St. Louis, which was the beginning of a life-long friendship between the two young dancers.

From Louisville, Patty went on to work in other burlesque theatres across the circuit, including Cincinnati, Chicago, and Kansas City, Kansas. In her earlier years, she preferred performing in the theatres where she got to meet many of the comics and work in the bits. As time passed, she preferred working in various clubs across the country.

She wrote, "It was so much easier to work in clubs, especially in California, where the shows started at 9:00 pm and closed at 2:00 am. Working in the theatre in Cincinnati, I remember starting at noon and dancing in six shows plus performing the bit parts, which lasted past midnight. It was way too strenuous."

When her husband got out of the service, the couple returned to San Francisco. Patty worked for Meyer Neff, but her marriage soon ended. Patty resumed her dancing career in Chicago clubs before returning to California for good in 1964, when she booked herself into the Roadhouse in West Sacramento. In between shows, she performed in a variety of clubs across the country. She remarried and settled down to raise four children. In Sacramento, she danced at the Driftwood and other clubs, but always returned to the Roadhouse, where she developed a close friendship with the owners and their family. Patty was known for twirling tassels. Her favorite number to perform to was "Wipe Out," and she could twirl up to four tassels at a time, or even while lying on her back.

Patty wrote, "I admired almost all the dancers, but always preferred to be different. However, I picked certain things I liked about some dancers and added those ideas to my show. I was privileged to see Sally Rand perform at the Roadhouse. Later, we met and worked together. I also got to see Evelyn West perform at a lounge in East St. Louis, and again I was so very impressed with the woman's performance."

Patty's parents were prominent members of Davis, California. Her father was head of the Electrical Engineering Department at the University of California, Davis campus, and her mother was a respected member of the local Bridge community. Patty's role in burlesque was a bit out of character for her family, but she was always honest and up front with them. When she first told her parents of her decision to become a dancer in burlesque, her mother simply wrote, "Go out and knock them dead, but be a lady about it!"

Patty wrote, "Mike Riaff was a jewel and a true gentleman. I was very, very shy. No one today believes that, but then it was true. I just wanted to dance so badly, but I didn't have enough lessons or experience to try out for other type shows or even chorus lines. For several years, the shows took up most of my life. There was no time for partying, although we'd all go out for an early breakfast after hours. During those years, my only friends were in show business, so we all thought alike. Some school friends might have had a problem with my performing in burlesque. I never hid it from them, but those who were sincere friends remained my friends. I was able to raise a family, and by working in burlesque, they had everything they needed, and they gave me everything I needed. My dream would be to revive burlesque and show those who were not there what this great art represented. I don't want it to become a lost art. It was a great life, and I have many happy memories. The girls I worked with were dedicated and good family people. I wouldn't have traded any part of my life in burlesque for anything; I was blessed to have had it in my life." Patty O'Farrell retired from burlesque in 1975.

Patty O'Farrell.
PHOTO COURTESY OF: PATTY O'FARRELL.

Julie Adorn.
PHOTO COURTESY OF: BURLESQUE HISTORICAL SOCIETY.

PEGGY LLOYD

She was an actress, songstress, and comedienne, who went on to emcee in burlesque clubs. Peggy wrote, "Long ago, I was the straight woman in the Frank Fay Revue at the Nora Bayes Theatre in New York City. That's when Lili St. Cyr slid from the balcony on a wire all the way to the stage, then took a bubble bath on stage."

After singing with Big Bands, performing in legitimate shows, and touring with the USO, Peggy went on to work one night at the Kandy Bar Club in West Palm Beach, and stayed for six years. She also worked burlesque clubs on the Grits Circuit before emceeing at the world-famous Palomino Club in Las Vegas. Peggy Lloyd had a long history in the world of entertainment before passing away in September 2004. She was a funny lady with a great voice and a big heart.

Peggy Lloyd.
PHOTO COURTESY
OF: PEGGY LLOYD.

PEPPER POWELL

Pepper was not an active member of the Burlesque Historical Society, although I occasionally heard from her. Her philosophy seemed to be that her days in burlesque were over and what lied ahead was more important. However, after I learned she died, her neighbor and good friend Ken Springer wrote and shared the following information with me.

"Pepper was born in Youngstown, Ohio, and raised by her grandparents. She left home at the age of fourteen. She danced in a chorus line for a while, but then discovered burlesque and knew it would pay much better. At the age of fifteen, Pepper was already 5' 8" and well-developed. That was the beginning of her theatre and nightclub career. When burlesque slackened off and became inelegant and vulgar, she decided to quit, but then Ann Corio asked her to join *This Was Burlesque* as one of the featured stars. Pepper liked that and was very proud to do it. She really loved performing. Pepper also loved animals. She owned several cats and a series of Yorkies." Ken also mentioned that Pepper had lots of friends, but was wary of getting "too involved." She was married once, but things did not work out, so she ended the marriage.

Pepper Powell. PHOTOS COURTESY OF: AL BAKER JR.

Pepper Powell.
PHOTO COURTESY OF: BURLESQUE
HISTORICAL SOCIETY.

Pepper Powell.
PHOTO COURTESY OF: BURLESQUE
HISTORICAL SOCIETY.

Peter Thomas also shared the following with me regarding Pepper's days in burlesque. "Among other places, Pepper Powell often worked the Gem Follies Theatre in Chicago. She stopped performing when the business got too dirty for her. Many features left the business for that reason. Pepper was a class act. She often worked on a circular platform that folded up into many hinged pieces about sixteen to eighteen inches from the floor. In spite of her classic features and sheer elegance, Pepper was a funny, witty girl." In May 2002, Pepper Powell died.

PETER "SONNY" THOMAS

Peter, an original member of The Golden Days of Burlesque Historical Society, grew up in Minneapolis, where he attended dance school. Making his debut in burlesque at the age of fifteen, he performed in big production numbers as an acrobatic tap dancer and singer.

Peter said, "I did many things. In some shows, I worked the scenes. In other shows, I sang. In some shows, I danced. There was never a dull moment. For a brief period, I even produced the girls' numbers. Later, the term became "choreographer," but it was "line producer" in my younger days." Peter described himself as "a thin singer, acrobatic tap-dancer, and actor. I guess I looked pretty good from the front of a theatre, even though I'm only 5' 8." Peter had a long, interesting career, and he has richly filled my days with stories regarding the golden days of burlesque. On February 8, 2008, those days ended when he passed away after a long illness.

Peter "Sonny" Thomas circa 1965, Chicago.
PHOTO COURTESY OF: PETER THOMAS.

RICKI COVETTE

She was known as the "World's Tallest Exotic at 6' 8." Ricki was born in Alberta, Canada, to American parents. At an early age, she left home to join the chorus line of one of Gypsy Rose Lee's touring revues. She soon found her way to New York City, where Lou Walters at the Latin Quarter Club encouraged her to become an exotic dancer. Growing up, Ricki felt her height was a hindrance, but she learned to use it to her advantage and featured it in her act.

"I did all the publicity venues, newspaper interviews, whatever it took to promote my act," she said. "All my routines were production numbers with a lot of props and a set."

Ricki mentioned that she also worked in the scenes during the first couple years she performed in burlesque. I can only imagine what that looked like. She had to have towered over everyone else who appeared in those bits.

Ricki recalled meeting Lois de Fee for the first time. "Lois was said to be the tallest exotic dancer working in burlesque during that time period. Lois looked up at Ricki and did not say a word; she just turned and walked away. I understand how Lois must have felt because I remember the first time I met Ricki and had to look up to the heavens to see her smiling face."

During her show business career, Ricki also worked in legitimate theatre road companies of *A Funny Thing Happened on the Way to the Forum* and *Marriage Go-Round,* as well as summer stock, television commercials, and the movie, *The Swingers.*

Ricki Covette.
PHOTO COURTESY
OF: RICKI COVETTE.

Ricki Covette. PHOTO COURTESY OF: RICKI COVETTE.

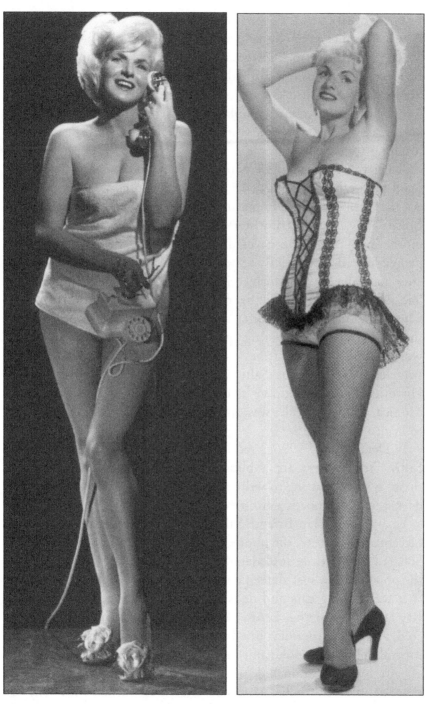

Ricki Covette. PHOTOS COURTESY OF: RICKI COVETTE.

SALLY MARR

In December 1994, Tanayo asked me to help find her old friend, "Boots Malloy," also known as Sally Marr. Sally, who was Lenny Bruce's mother, was not difficult to locate, and I always enjoyed our phone conversations. As soon as I picked up the phone, I knew who was calling, due to her Brooklyn-Jewish accent. She could have been reading *Dick and Jane* stories for all it mattered; I just enjoyed listening to her talk.

A native of Jamaica, New York, Sally worked as a waitress and maid before becoming a dancer and stand-up comedienne. In her act, she often performed impressions of Jimmy Cagney and Humphrey Bogart. I was told Lenny started his own career by imitating his mother's routines. She never discussed Lenny with me, but other people have mentioned that she often said she thought Lenny took after her. Sally Marr performed in nightclubs, television, and movies. She also worked as a talent agent and was credited with discovering Cheech and Chong, Pat Morita, and Sam Kiniston. As "Boots Malloy," she ran a school for young, potential exotic dancers, as well as worked as a choreographer and emcee in some of the old Los Angeles area strip clubs. Sally came to our June 26, 1995 Burlesque Historical Society reunion held at Betty Rowland's club in Santa Monica, California. She was unable to attend future gatherings due to health issues.

In December of 1996, I received my last hand-written note from Sally. "Your letters are a blessing," she wrote. "Please continue them. It's hard for me to write and I'm not writing to anyone these days, but I love hearing from you."

For the next year, I wrote Sally notes every other week. Then on December 15, 1997, the phone call came telling me of Sally's death. She had passed away at Cedars-Sinai Medical Center in Los Angeles the previous day, just sixteen days short of her ninety-first birthday.

It was raining cats and dogs on the day of her funeral. Frankie Ray later told me that Lenny's services were held on a very similar, cold, wet, and rainy day, but I think Sally would have enjoyed her funeral. The Rabi spoke and then announced, "If anyone wants to say anything, stand up and speak." There must have been twenty or more people who spoke. Most had known or worked with Sally for years. Some told funny stories; others told very touching stories. It was sad, yet light-hearted, and very apparent that Sally Marr had many friends who loved her deeply.

Sally Marr.
PHOTO COURTESY OF: FRANKIE RAY.

Tanayo.
AUTHORS COLLECTION.

SANDRA ELLIS

In 1936, Sandra, a native New Yorker, auditioned for *Minsky's Burlesque* after seeing an ad in a local New York newspaper. She was hired immediately. She danced at Billy Minsky's Republic Theatre on 42nd Street and Broadway, at the Continental Theatre, and at the beautiful Oriental Theatre at 52nd Street and Broadway. When Minsky took over the world famous Apollo Theatre at 125th Street, it was briefly renamed the Tri-Borough Theatre, but later renamed the Apollo Theatre.

Sandra wriote, "I worked with Robert Alda and remember when Alan was a two-year-old child. We all played with him in-between show times. The Minsky organization supplied the costumes for the showgirls and chorus. The single acts, also known as strippers, supplied their own costumes. I also did blackout bits with Harry Lavine. Harry's daughter was La Vodis, and her husband was Billy Ainsley. Margie Hart, Gladys Fox, Hinda Wassau, Julie Bryan, Rags Ragland, and Electra, are just a few that I worked with. I preferred working theatres and opposed the clubs. My favorite music was "Twilight in Turkey," "Mood Indigo," "Stairway to the Stars," and "Stay in My Arms Cinderella." Eddie Lynch was the choreographer, and I only worked for the Minsky's." Sandra Ellis remained with the Minsky Organization until the City of New York closed down all the burlesque theatres.

Burlesque Artists Ass'n Membership Card belonging to Sandra Ellis for the season-running through October 31,1939.
PHOTO COURTESY OF: SANDRA ELLIS.

Sandra Ellis.
PHOTO COURTESY OF: SANDRA ELLIS.

Sandy O'Hara

Known as "The Improper Bostonian," Sandy continues to star in, *The Best of Burlesque*. Starting her career at the age of seventeen in the chorus line, she was headlining *Minsky's Burlesque Follies* in Las Vegas by the age of twenty. Sandy also starred in Ann Corio's, *This Was Burlesque*, Barry Ashton's, *Wonderful World of Burlesque*, and Rocky Senne's *Wild World of Burlesque*. Sandy is a world-renowned fan dancer known for her tribute to Sally Rand. After a 1970 appearance at Nellis Air Force Base in Las Vegas during the Vietnam War, Miss O'Hara was dubbed, "Miss Armed Forces Pin-Up." She was the first lady so honored since Marilyn Monroe was bestowed the honor during the Korean Conflict. Sandy married David Hanson, the creator, producer, director, and writer of, *The Best of Burlesque*. Together, they run D & S Productions. Although born into a show business family, David spent nine years as a professional baseball player before actively becoming involved in show business as an actor, stunt man, stand-up comedian, writer, and director. David says, "My first love has always been the wacky world of burlesque comedy."

David Hanson.
Photo courtesy of: Sandy O'Hara and David Hanson.

Sandy O'Hara.
PHOTOS COURTESY
OF: SANDY O'HARA
AND DAVID HANSON.

SATIN DOLL

In 1959, "Satin Doll #7," as she calls herself, began her career in burlesque by appearing at the Terris Club in Milwaukee, where she performed a soft-shoe and dance routine. Billed as, "The Fabulous Dee Dee," "DeAnna Day," "Princess Dee," or "Satin Doll," she learned the artsy-seductive moves from such troupers as The Gypsy, Mitzi, Tanya, and other high-caliber artists in the world of burlesque. She worked mostly in the Midwest, but did appear in clubs and theatres across the United States, including Jack Ruby's Club in Dallas. She performed as a dancer, comedienne, and emcee. In 1969, she retired to enjoy a new career as a nationally published author of romance, poetry, and children's books.

Satin Doll.
AUTHORS COLLECTION.

SEQUIN

Her career in show business first began at age of seventeen, when she was hired as a nightclub singer in Oakland, California. The only gown she had to wear was her high school prom dress. During 1945, the war brought swarms of sailors to Oakland. They did not care what a gal was wearing as long as she was good-looking. By the time Sequin was nineteen, she had performed for the USO, as well as numerous Veterans Hospitals, as she made her way across the country to join Buddy Johnson's band in New York City. After touring with Johnson and later Jack "Madman" Mitchell, Sequin, with the aid of her friend and artist Ted Littleton, created a striptease act and began her burlesque career at Strip City in Los Angeles. Lili St Cyr was her role model.

Sequin wrote, "When I lived in New York with Ted, Conductor John Williams was a frequent visitor, but he was known as Johnny Williams then and he was a jazz pianist. I met some truly fabulous people, all old-timers, but definitely good- timers. Miles Davis lived in my apartment building, and Bobby Hackett, the trumpet player, was a good friend. There was also Davey Lambert of Lambert, Hendricks, and Ross, Oscar Pettiford, the jazz cellist, Bill Crow, the bassist, and Chet Baker, a trumpet player like no other."

Touring as "Sequin, Beauty to the 4th Dimension," she worked throughout the United States in theatres and clubs. Dick Richards, the dancer turned agent was instrumental in booking Sequin onto the Ohio Burlesque Circuit until she appeared at Minsky's in 1957. There, she met future husband Tony Tamburello. Tony, musical director for Tony Bennett, created a nightclub routine with special material which he and Sequin performed until they married a year later and Sequin retired.

Over the years, Sequin met many entertainers. She wrote, "I met Judy Garland at her daughter Lorna's sweet sixteen party. We were there with Tony Bennett, and my husband was playing the piano. All of a sudden, he went into the introduction to one of my numbers, and I just automatically started singing the first line. I wasn't aware that he was going to do that—not in front of Judy Garland, but he did. I had to respond. Talk about butterflies!"

Sequin.
Photos courtesy of: Sequin.

SHEILA RAE

From 1946 to 1971, Sheila Rae worked in burlesque. She was a feature attraction, who performed in clubs and theatres all over the United States, Europe, and Canada. She was sometimes billed as "The Hungarian Bombshell."

Sheila Rae.
PHOTO COURTESY OF: SHEILA RAE.

Sheila Rae.
Photos courtesy of: Sheila Rae.

SHERRY BRITTON

At age fifteen, an agent suggested that Sherry audition for a burlesque show. She landed her first job in the chorus line at the People's Theatre on the Bowery in New York. A week later, she was a principal. The youngster may have been fifteen, but she had the figure of a twenty-year-old. For five years, she toured the country on various burlesque circuits. For seven and a half years, Sherry starred at the world famous Leon & Eddie's nightclub in New York City.

As a popular pin-up model during World War Two, Sherry often performed and counseled on ships, camps, and in hospitals. For this service, President Franklin D. Roosevelt bestowed upon her the rank of Honorary Brigadier General. After leaving Leon & Eddie's, Sherry performed during winter months in all the top nightclubs in major cities across the United States. She appeared on the straw-hat theatre circuit during summers. She appeared on Broadway in several shows, including opposite John Garfield in *Peer Gynt, Drink to Me Only*, which was directed by George Abbott, and in 1957, opposite Tom Poston in *The Best of Burlesque* at the Carnegie Hall Playhouse. That show was then made into an MGM album that Georgia Sothern sent to Ann Corio. In the 1960s, Corio took the show on the road and made a fortune with it. Sherry's company sued, but Ann changed the name to *This Was Burlesque*, which threw out the lawsuit. Sherry has also appeared on many television shows, but her favorite role was as Adelaide in *Guys and Dolls*.

At age fifty-three, Sherry married Robert Gross, the love of her life. At the age of sixty three, she graduated pre-law, Magna Cum Laude from Fordham University. In 2003, Sherry celebrated her eighty-fifth birthday with a gala affair at The National Arts Club, which included performing *Vintage Sherry*, her own one-woman show that she wrote. Besides occasional performances, Sherry remained very active, and she was busy writing her memoirs when she passed away on April 15th, 2008.

Sherry Britton. PHOTO COURTESY OF: SHERRY BRITTON.

Sherry Britton.
PHOTO COURTESY OF: MARINKA.

Sherry Britton.
PHOTO COURTESY OF: SHERRY BRITTON.

STACY FARRELL

Also known as "Eartha Quake," Stacy began her career in burlesque in the chorus line at the Follies Theatre in Los Angeles when she was nineteen years old. At that time the chorus line consisted of about twenty girls.

Stacy told me, "In the old days, in order to work in burlesque, you had to know how to dance. We did everything: tap, ballet, toe, and jazz. We had to parade around the stage with grace, always smiling at the audience. We also had to do scenes with the comics. This gave us all-around experience to go on and do many other things."

Stacy loved being a dancer and working in the chorus line. She developed many close friendships that she maintained over the years, including friendships with women who started their careers dancing in that same chorus line. Stacy also talked of dancers she met at the theatre who could not even walk to music until choreographer Lillian Hunt, worked with them. As time went by, Stacy became a feature in burlesque working in theatres and clubs. When working on the West coast, she worked as "Stacy Farrell."

Stacy Farrell.
PHOTO COURTESY OF:
STACY FARRELL.

Stacy Farrell.
PHOTO COURTESY OF: STACY FARRELL.

When working on the East coast, Alaska, Hawaii, and Japan, Stacy performed as "Eartha Quake." Stacy's career as a dancer spanned five decades, beginning in the 1930s and ending in 1974, when told she had to appear nude in clubs. After a long illustrious career on some of the biggest and best burlesque stages, Stacy was not interested in performing in the nude. On November 14, 2005, Stacy Farrell passed away.

SUE MARTIN

In 1954, Sue began her career in burlesque. She primarily performed on the West coast and Hawaii, but also worked in the Midwest and in Belgium. Either billed as "Miss Park Avenue" or "Lady of Temptation," Sue was known as much for her comedy and quick wit as her beautiful figure and ability to tease. She preferred working clubs to the theatre circuit, where her talents as an emcee and comedienne were showcased. Sue also appeared on television and radio programs, including, *The Jack Paar Show*. In 1986, Sue Martin retired, and in October 2007, she passed away.

Sue Martin. PHOTO COURTESY OF: SUE MARTIN.

Sue Martin.
PHOTOS COURTESY OF:
SUE MARTIN.

SUNNY DARE

At the age of seventeen, Bobbie Rogers joined the chorus line at the Gayety Theatre in Detroit, which was just the beginning of a long, successful career in burlesque. In 1950, she went on the road with Sally Rand. In 1951, she changed her name to "Sunny Dare" and was billed as "The Girl with the Blue Hair." Sunny performed as a feature all over the United States, as well as touring Japan. She would sing, perform acrobatics, high jumps, and splits. Working for Minsky's in the late 1960s, she worked month-long club shows in Italy, England, and the Dominican Republic. In 1970, she saw where burlesque was headed and decided to make a change. She went to nursing school by day, and performed by night as Nejma, "Turkey's Foremost Belly Dancer." For years, she worked as a belly dancer in Greek clubs and Middle Eastern restaurants, while working her way through nursing school. Sunny proudly admits that, as a dancer, she would try anything. However, she never took it all off and she never got arrested.

Sunny was a part of The Golden Days of Burlesque Historical Society since the group was formed, but in 2006, she joined us for her first reunion. I learned what a character she truly was, and I asked her help in writing a full chapter for this book. Sunny Dare died on August 8, 2008.

Sunny Dare. PHOTO COURTESY OF: SUNNY DARE.

Nejma, also known as Sunny Dare.
AUTHORS COLLECTION.

Sunny Dare.
PHOTO COURTESY OF: JONI TAYLOR.

Sunny Dare.
PHOTO COURTESY
OF: SUNNY DARE.

SUNNY DAY

It was shortly after being introduced to the owner of the Follies Theatre in Baltimore that Sunny began her career in burlesque. Once her routines were polished and perfected at the Follies, she hit the road. Being able to travel appealed to her the most. Performing in clubs and theatres across the United States and Canada, Sunny was known for her "Butterfly" act. The finale included wings that spread open to approximately twenty feet. In 1976, Sunny retired from burlesque to pursue a career in acting and expand her interest in photography.

Sunny Day.
PHOTOS COURTESY OF: SUNNY DAY.

SUNNY KNIGHT

Originally from Arkansas, Sunny began her show business career as a model for Power's Modeling Agency. She worked her way into bit parts in movies, small roles in stage productions on Broadway, and performed as an Earl Carroll showgirl. Eventually, she went on to become half of the dance team, Sonia and Rene, performing primarily in Mexico.

In a February 19, 1952 newspaper column, Dorothy Kilgallen wrote that Sunny had been ordered by a psychoanalyst to take up strip teasing to "solve her conflicts." In a separate story appearing in another newspaper, it was reported that Sunny had only a short time to live. It was certainly all a gimmick, but it started Sunny Knight's career in burlesque. She was billed as "The Girl of the Golden West," and performed all over the United States, Canada, Japan, Mexico, and the Philippines. No matter where she worked, it was always made very clear that she did not mix with the customers.

Sunny Knight and unknowns in a comedy bit. Can anyone help us identify the fellows? PHOTO COURTESY OF: LORRAINE LEE.

Sunny always worked to better herself as an individual. She took singing lessons in the morning, dancing lessons in the afternoon, as well as studied a variety of languages and creative writing. She often worked with emcee Bob Hansen, and was life-long friends with Lorraine Lee, who provided photos and information about Sunny for our archives. Lorraine also told me of a song written about Sunny entitled, "When Sunny Gets Blue." Marvin Fisher wrote the music, Jack Segal the lyrics, and many, including Johnny Mathis, Nat "King" Cole, and Ella Fitzgerald recorded the song. Sunny Knight remained active all of her life, had one of those infectious laughs, and was always great fun to talk to. She passed away in March 1997.

Sunny Knight.
PHOTO COURTESY OF: BURLESQUE HISTORICAL SOCIETY.

Sunny Knight.
PHOTOS COURTESY OF: LORRAINE LEE.

Sunny Knight with friend, emcee Bob Hansen.
PHOTO COURTESY OF: LORRAINE LEE.

TAFFEY O'NEIL

From 1953 to 1972, Taffey performed on burlesque stages all across the United States as a headliner. After her first year of dancing, Taffey actually preferred working supper clubs to theatres and nightclubs. When asked why, she said, "It was always couples who came to supper clubs to see the shows together. Supper clubs presented more of a family atmosphere, and the shows presented a variety of entertainment."

Taffey O'Neil.
PHOTO COURTESY OF: BURLESQUE HISTORICAL SOCIETY.

Normally dancing on the West coast to be near her family, Taffey did spend all of 1963 on the road. However, she only appeared on the East coast and Midwest burlesque circuits four times during her career. When asked about her billing, she stated, "I never used anything but my name." Lili St. Cyr's name was mentioned when asked if there were any dancers she admired, but Taffey went on to say that she "never idolized any one particular dancer."

Taffey O'Neil.

Taffey O'Neil has been a part of The Golden Days of Burlesque Historical Society since the group was formed in 1995. She and her husband have attended nearly every reunion, and they are "family."

TANAYO

Billed as "The Costa Rican Dream Girl," Tanayo was the reason the Burlesque Historical Society was created. In December 1994, her body already showing signs of disease, Tanayo asked me to help find friends she had performed with in burlesque. Once I agreed to help, she provided me with what information she had, and the search began. Most of her addresses were old, or many were simply listed under stage names. That was the beginning of The Golden Days of Burlesque Historical Society.

Tanayo was a war bride, who came to this country unable to read, write, or even speak much English. Trapped in an abusive marriage, she turned her talents and energy towards dancing on the burlesque stage. Burlesque became her life, as she danced primarily

Tanayo.
PHOTO COURTESY OF: GUSSIE GROSS.

on the West coast, but occasionally back east as well. Over the years, Tanayo taught herself to speak English, as well as to read and write. Despite her religious beliefs, she divorced her husband and remarried. She was an intelligent woman with a big heart and was always giving her time to others.

Tanayo was not well for many years, but she was never one to complain. This lady always wanted to find and reconnect with friends from burlesque and keep the history alive. Although never well enough to attend the Las Vegas reunions, she was a regular, who came to the reunions held in California. There was limited communication with her over the last few years of her life due to her illness. In August of 2003, we finally lost Tanayo.

Tanayo.
PHOTO COURTESY OF: GUSSIE GROSS.

TANYA

Tanya, along with sisters Bronya and Marie Stobbe, all performed in burlesque. Tanya wrote, "We started out dancing as kids. As children in school, we put on shows at our home on Saturday afternoons. We showed movies, recited poetry, and performed shadow shows on a large sheet hung in the living room. We also did tap routines and my version of a hula. I was only ten years old, but that was our beginning in show biz. After studying tap, ballet, adagio, and acrobatics, my sisters and I danced all over town on Saturday night, getting experience. Thank heaven for dancing schools in the 1930s."

In the late 1930s after Bronya graduated from high school, she left home to dance in nightclubs in Kansas City and Missouri, and she worked all across the United States and Canada. Bronya was best known for her half-and-half act, and always felt as though dancing was her life. In November 1995, she passed away.

Marie also left home to dance, but had to stay and finish schooling. Marie preferred dancing in vaudeville shows in Chicago and New York theatres. Her dancing troupe also traveled to Mexico. In November 1998, she passed away.

Marie Stobbe.
PHOTO COURTESY
OF: TANYA.

TOP LEFT:
Bronya.
PHOTOS COURTESY OF:
TANYA.

TOP RIGHT:
Tanya.
PHOTOS COURTESY OF:
TANYA.

LEFT:
Bronya performing her Dance of Lovers routine.
PHOTO COURTESY OF:
TANYA.

Bronya.
Photos courtesy of: Tanya.

Tanya wrote the following about her own career in burlesque. "I preferred to dance in nightclubs, and started my professional career in the late 1940s in Kansas City, Missouri. I traveled from the Midwest to the East coast, working in Chicago, New Orleans, Rhode Island, and Florida. While dancing in Florida, I performed under the name "Dee Valka." Routines I performed included the "Jungle Dance," where I used a leopard costume, fluorescent material and black lights. In the "Dance of the Lovers," I appeared in an optical illusion as a half-man and half-woman. The half-and-half act was always popular with the crowds. I also performed a fan dance using large, gorgeous, blue ostrich plumes. I stopped dancing in the 1960s."

TERI STARR

Teri wrote, "I started stripping in 1960. I worked a short time, only about three months, and then quit. I didn't like it at first, but it was so much easier than being a hairdresser. So I began dancing again part-time when someone wanted to take time off at the clubs. I did that for about five years, and then started to dance full time in Las Vegas. I loved it the second time around. Unfortunately, I started too late to really work with all the big stars of burlesque, but I loved the freedom of traveling. Universal Studios sent me to Japan twice, once to do a two-part travelogue for television. Then, I went to Egypt, where I worked at the Hilton and Sheraton Hotels with the existing shows. It was the most fun time in my life. I loved entertaining and wish there was something comedic that I could do to go back on stage!"

Teri, interested in spiritual studies all of her life, became a licensed minister. Her hobbies included painting, cooking, and traveling. She spent a year in Canada, and she visited Peru, Israel, and twice went to Japan and Egypt.

Teri Starr.
PHOTO COURTESY
OF: TERI STARR.

Teri Starr.
PHOTO COURTESY
OF: TERI STARR.

TONY MIDNITE

A true legend in the field of female impersonation, Tony went on to design and create elaborate sequin-embroidered gowns and costumes for some of the biggest names in burlesque, including Marion Russell, Evelyn West, June Harlow, Lois de Fee, Gay Dawn, Rita Atlanta, Patti Waggin, Pepper Powell, Tina Christine, April March, Rusty Lane, Grace Reed, Ann Perri, Lila Turner, Penny Carlton, Suzanne Pritchard, and Christina, "The Bronze Goddess." From 1952 to 1978, his Chicago studio was located near the nightclub district.

Tony was born in Texas in 1926. He worked at Hunter's Point Navy Yard near San Francisco during World War Two, when he used a fake ID to see the world-famous revue of female impersonators at Finocchio's. While watching the show, Tony felt confident that he could perform as well, or better. After the war, he began his career as a female impersonator at the Granada Club in Galveston, Texas. He went on to play clubs across the country before joining the renowned Jewel Box Revue in 1948. At that time, Broadway designer Stanley Rogers, created the costumes for the show. When he discovered that Tony made his own costumes, Rogers asked him to be his assistant. Tony seized the opportunity to learn from a true professional and to perfect his craft.

After four years with the revue, Tony signed on as a performer at the Miami Lounge in Chicago. He loved the Chicago nightlife. There was Minsky's Rialto Burlesque, as well as the Follies, the Gaiety Theatre, and a score of strip clubs in the area. Several of the dancers lived in his hotel.

"I got to know them," Tony said, "and when they found out that I could sew, they began to ask me to make things for them. Marion Russell was my first customer. The valet shop at the hotel was empty, so I rented and re-decorated it, then opened my first studio. In a very short time, I had to hire help to take care of all my orders. I got a sequin embroidery machine from Paris and specialized in very elaborate embroidered gowns and costumes. I gave the girls costumes that they never dreamed of owning. Several agents even began to send me their dancers because they could get them more money if they had my gowns. First, they would get a gown; then they had photos made by Maurice Seymour. From then on, their future bookings were assured."

In 1958, Danny Brown brought the Jewel Box Revue to Roberts Show Club in South Chicago. They packed the club from day one, and Danny asked Tony to create new costumes for the entire show. Tony designed some of the most elaborate costumes ever seen on a stage. The show performed in Chicago for eight record-breaking months, and when they left, Tony toured with the revue as emcee. The revue, seen in the Catskills by the Schubert's, was booked for Broadway. During the Broadway run, Tony's costumes brought him several offers, so he decided to stay in New York. He created costumes for the 82 Club and several road shows including *Gypsy* and *Subways are for Sleeping* for producer David Merrick. Tony also worked on the *Perry Como Show* on television and on several productions at the Metropolitan Opera, most notably *Cleopatra*.

Tony Midnite, 1957. On September 1st, 2009, Tony died; the last of the great old-time costume makers.
PHOTO COURTESY OF: TONY MIDNITE.

Tony Midnite in drag; Chicago, 1953.
PHOTO COURTESY OF: TONY MIDNITE.

Penny Carlton appearing in Tony Midnite creations.
PHOTOS COURTESY OF: TONY MIDNITE.

Suzanne Pritchard wearing her own Tony Midnite creation.
PHOTO COURTESY OF: TONY MIDNITE.

In 1964, Tony was overworked and homesick for Chicago. He moved back to the windy city and opened a studio in the Chicago Theatre building. As the years went by, the strip clubs closed, as did Minsky's Rialto Theatre. Tony held on through 1978, when he officially retired as a costumer.

"I didn't know what an eight-hour shift was," he wrote. "You know, in show business, there were always deadlines to meet."

In 1981, he moved to Las Vegas where he works on a book of his memoirs.

VAL VALENTINE

Val studied dance as a kid. In 1955, she began her exotic dancing career by traveling with Mitzi, her mom's best friend, and working in the carnival chorus line for Raynell Golden on the Cetlin and Wilson Shows. Tutored by Mitzi, she soon became a feature act, with costumes made by Tony Midnite. By 1958, Val Valentine was a headliner on the burlesque theatre circuit. Through the late 1970s, Val, often billed as "Cupid's Cutie," or "Anatomy Award Winner," worked carnival revues during summers and falls, and burlesque clubs and theatres the rest of the year. She retired in 1986 from performing on all burlesque stages.

The Golden Days of Burlesque Historical Society members were asked at one time to send a listing of people they worked with, as well as theatres where they performed. Val responded, and these are burlesque theatres where she worked:

THE RIO, SACRAMENTO, CALIFORNIA
THE CASINO, TORONTO, CANADA
THE MELODY, NEW YORK CITY
THE CIVIC, SYRACUSE, NEW YORK
THE GARDEN, COLUMBUS, OHIO
THE RITZ, INDIANAPOLIS, INDIANA
THE ALVIN, MINNEAPOLIS, MINNESOTA
THE EMPIRE, NEWARK, NEW JERSEY
THE MAYFAIR, DAYTON, OHIO
THE LYRIC, ALLENTOWN, PENNSYLVANIA
THE GAYETY, DETROIT, MICHIGAN
THE FOX, INDIANAPOLIS, INDIANA
THE GAYETY, CINCINNATI, OHIO
THE GAYETY, PITTSBURGH, PENNSYLVANIA
THE ROXY, CLEVELAND, OHIO
THE MONROE, KEY WEST, FLORIDA
THE HUDSON, UNION CITY, NEW JERSEY
THE LEE, RICHMOND, VIRGINIA
THE PARK, YOUNGSTOWN, OHIO
THE GAYETY, WASHINGTON, D.C.
THE FOLLIES, SAN FRANCISCO, CALIFORNIA
THE TOWN HALL, TOLEDO, OHIO

The Casino, Boston, Maryland
The Gayety, Baltimore, Maryland
The Troc, Philadelphia, Pennsylvania
The Mayfair, New York City
The Gayety, New York City
The Paris, Miami Beach, Florida
The Gayety, Miami Beach, Florida
The Pussycat, Miami, Florida
The Esquire, Toledo, Ohio
The Palace, Buffalo, New York
The Folly, Kansas City, Missouri
The Follies, Chicago, Illinois
The Savoy, Louisville, Kentucky
The Grand, St. Louis, Missouri
The World, St. Louis, Missouri
The Grand Theatre, in Canton, Ohio

Val Valentine. Authors Collection.

Val Valentine.
PHOTO COURTESY OF: VAL VALENTINE.

Val Valentine.
PHOTO COURTESY OF: VAL VALENTINE.

VICKI O'DAY

From 1964 to 1979, Vicki mostly danced in the burlesque clubs on the West coast, but also in Alaska and Canada. She liked to tell how she was headed to Guam to perform, and made a left turn only to find herself dancing in Boston instead. She was also known as "Astarte, Goddess of Fertility." In 1965, Vicki made *A Day in the Life of a Stripper*, a movie shot in Denver with Tempest Storm.

Vicki O'Day.
PHOTOS COURTESY OF: VICKI O'DAY.

ZORITA

In 1934, while selling cigarettes at the New York State Fair, young Katherine Boyd spent the week watching a dancer in *The Streets of Paris* Show perform what was known as a "sleeve dance." Studying movements and making mental notes on everything she observed, Katherine then bought a pair of long, black gloves and the items needed to make a similar, yet much simpler costume. After creating her costume, she walked into the 830 Club, a nightclub owned by the Capone's. Katherine proceeded to tell the owner she was the sleeve dancer from the fair and she was looking for a job.

Capone asked, "How much?"

"$125 a week," she replied.

He hired her, and that was her first job in burlesque.

Katherine's next job was at the California Pacific International Exposition in San Diego. The attraction that fascinated her most was an Adam and Eve show run by an elderly gentleman. During the run of the fair the old man and young woman became friends. Although she was frightened at first, he gave her a large snake and taught her how to handle him.

On the last day of the fair, Katherine was offered a job in a San Francisco theatre. She was asked to perform a dance number with a large white veil, and was to be called "Zorita." Every four weeks, the producer changed the show. Learning that Katherine owned a large snake, he suggested she and her snake perform in a production number. That was the beginning of Zorita performing with a snake in her routine.

"All my snakes were named Oscar or Elmer," she wrote. "They were boa constrictors. My snake routine was a good number. It was sexy and very effective."

Zorita had a long career in burlesque preferring clubs to theatres. After working all over the United States, she settled down in Florida. She owned a successful club in Miami Beach for several years before deciding to retire. Zorita was one of the original members of The Golden Days of Burlesque Historical Society. She died in November 2001.

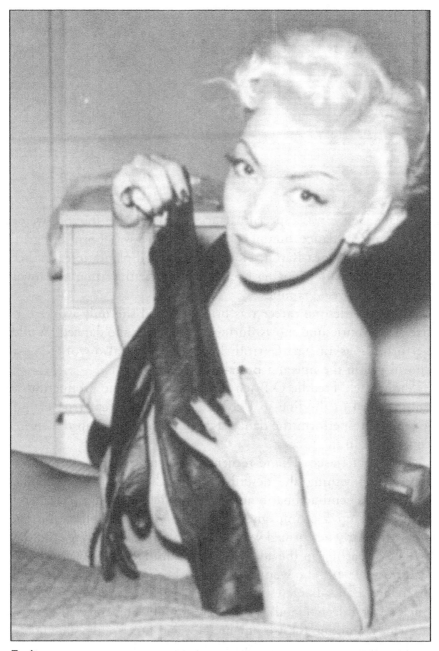

Zorita.
Photo courtesy of: Zorita.

Diane De Lys
"The Devil and the Virgin"

Diane De Lys was a specialty dancer known for her interpretive or dramatic dance numbers. In 1916, she was born Imogene Alice Gates in Boca Raton, Florida, on a small plantation that her parents settled after moving from Vermont. At that time, the town consisted of twelve families.

Diane's burlesque career was brief; she said she only worked in five actual burlesque shows during all the years she danced. While performing as an Earl Carroll showgirl, Diane also worked as a chorus girl in the line at a Buffalo, New York theatre.

She wrote, "Freddie O'Brien was in charge of the production. I only worked in the line so I could learn a time step. I never did learn how to perform the dance step and just messed up the entire chorus line in the process."

After that fiasco, Diane returned to performing a solo dance routine, something she described as "a champagne waltz." The dance was a semi-acrobatic number in which she did a back bend and picked up a champagne glass in her teeth. Another routine Diane regularly performed was an oriental cymbal number, and she was also a partner in the adagio dance team, Don and Diane.

Around 1940, she went to Paris to become a showgirl at the legendary Folies-Bergere. From there, she went on at work in England at Eileen Hood's famous Windmill. She traveled abroad frequently, working theatres, nightclubs, and hotels, but came home to the United States at the start of World War Two.

After seeing a half-and-half act, Diane created a dramatic dance routine she called "The Devil and the Virgin." This was the number for which she was best-known.

"I did a few strip numbers, as I became popular in the 1950s in the clubs," she later recalled. "I never did any bumps and grinds; I never did anything raunchy. Most of my numbers involved props, and I had it written into my contract that I didn't mix with the customers."

Diane spent twenty-seven years working as a dancer and performer, which included working in a few films. She also trained some younger dancers, who were just breaking into show business, such as Marie Angel, Joan Collier, and Jeanne Christian. In 1960, her last professional photographs as a dancer were taken.

Over the years, Diane and Sally Rand became close friends. Sally often stayed at Diane's Coral Gables home while working in Florida. When asked about others she knew, worked with, or with whom she remained friendly, Diane recalled, "To me, Lili St. Cyr was all class—one of the best. Once, I followed her at the Palm Club in Palm Beach. She was a beautiful dancer."

Diane also remained close friends with Meleana Dorn, until Dorn passed away in 1998. Meleana began her career as a Polynesian belly dancer, and then went on to perform as an exotic dancer in burlesque. Diane also mentioned knowing Daisy and Violet Hilton when they all worked together in Buffalo, New York, back in the 1940s. Diane helped with their costumes by splitting open new gowns and then sewing them together again, to fit more appropriately. Janeen, billed as "The Electric Tassel Queen," and her husband, Joe Rio, were also close friends from show business. Never a party girl, and always quite shy, Diane stayed in touch with few people.

After retiring from the stage, Diane continued to lead an active life. In 1965, she and her husband opened the Chez Joey, a popular restaurant in Boca Raton, but their marriage did not survive. In 1969, Diane was involved in a serious car accident. During her year of recovery, she went searching for answers to the deep questions about life. She took courses in Psychology, Parapsychology, and Addiction Research. Deciding she could only help herself by helping others, Diane opened a counseling center. She spoke at churches, schools, prisons, and AA meetings. Diane also drove a taxicab, wrote children's stories, many other short stories, a play, and a history on Boca Raton, Florida.

She loves history in general, and continues to write what she can about her own personal history. Because her family was one of the first to settle the area in which she lives, she remains as active as possible with the local historical society. Diane continues to study alternative healing methods, grow orchids and other plants, and loves all types of animals. She has a big heart, which sometimes gets her in trouble, yet she continues to grow with age. She greets everyone she sees with a smile, and she has a sense of humor to match. One never knows what Diane will be busy doing; for she is not one to remain still for long.

Diane De Lys.
Photo courtesy of: Diane De Lys.

RIGHT:
Al Hirshfeld drawing of Diane in 1944.
PHOTO COURTESY OF: DIANE DE LYS.

BELOW:
"My First Costume."
PHOTO COURTESY OF: DIANE DE LYS.

BELOW RIGHT:
Diane De Lys Flyer.
PHOTO COURTESY OF: DIANE DE LYS.

Diane De Lys.

ABOVE:
Diane De Lys.
PHOTO COURTESY
OF: DIANE DE LYS.

ABOVE RIGHT:
Marie Angel.
PHOTO COURTESY
OF: DIANE DE LYS.

RIGHT:
Diane De Lys.
PHOTO COURTESY
OF: DIANE DE LYS.

Daisy and Violet Hilton

On February 5, 1908, Daisy and Violet Hilton were born in England to Kate Skinner, a young, unwed barmaid, but they were adopted by Mary Hilton. The sisters, who were Siamese twins, were born joined together near the base of their spine at the hip and shared blood circulation, but no major organs. Soon after acquiring the twins, they were exhibited in circuses and fairs across the United States and Europe. When the girls were not being displayed in sideshows, Mary, along with her sixth and final husband, Meyer Meyers, rigorously trained them in singing, dancing, piano, violin, clarinet, and the saxophone. The twins lived with the Meyers' in a mansion in San Antonio, Texas until the early 1930s.

The sisters eventually developed a vaudeville act, which debuted at Loew's State Theatre in Newark, New Jersey, in February 1925. The twins, relying solely on their talents, soon became a big hit playing musical instruments and performing dance routines. Touring the circuit with their act, "The Hilton Sisters' Revue," Daisy and Violet Hilton were billed as "The Eighth Wonder of the World."

When Mary died, her husband and daughter continued to manage the sisters' act, but in 1931, the twins filed a lawsuit and were awarded their independence. They left the sideshow circuit for good. In 1932, the twins appeared as themselves in the movie, *Freaks*. The film exploited those appearing in sideshows, and when re-released in the 1960s, the film became a cult classic.

Supposedly, the Hilton sisters were notorious for their many sexual adventures and affairs, often competing against one another for men. Both Daisy and Violet married, but neither had children and each marriage lasted only a short time. In 1936, Violet married James Walker Moore at the Texas Centennial Exposition in Dallas. The Moore's wedding followed a long series of marriage license applications Violet had filed, each with different men in over twenty different states. Under heavy publicity, those applications were all denied for reasons of "morality of public decency." In 1941, Daisy married dancer Buddy Sawyer in Buffalo, New York. Their marriage lasted two weeks.

Versions depicting the sisters' early lives are questionable, since true-life pamphlets handed out at shows misrepresented their childhood. However, according to the sisters' 1942 autobiography, Mary Hilton's successive husbands were physically abusive.

As the years progressed, the public lost interest in the sisters and they settled in Miami. Several stories existed about them. One claimed that the sisters ran a fruit stand; another said they ran a hamburger stand called the Hilton Sister's Snack Bar. Whatever business it was, it failed, and they turned to Hollywood.

In 1950, the sisters appeared in the film, *Chained for Life*, and when *Freaks* was re-released in the 1960s, the sisters went on a national tour to help with the publicity. Their last public appearance was in North Carolina at a drive-in movie theatre. The man who set up the tour promised them transportation following their appearance. He never showed up, leaving the sisters penniless and stranded. To survive, Daisy and Violet took a job at a local grocery store. One worked the register and the other bagged groceries. In early January 1969, the twins failed to report for work and were found dead in their home. The theatrical musical, *Side Show*, first performed in 1997, was loosely based on the sisters' lives.

Daisy Hilton once said, "We don't mind having people stare at us. We're used to it. We've never known anything else."

After the late Peter Thomas wrote to me that the sisters worked in burlesque, I obtained positive proof from Connie Fanslau's estate. From the 1930s to the 1950s, Connie was an exotic dancer. Photographs purchased from her estate included marquee photos and a photo of Daisy and Violet Hilton. The women worked together on the burlesque circuit back in 1937. It all tied-in with Diane De Lys' account of working with the sisters and Peter's story, as well.

Peter wrote, "Siamese twins, Daisy and Violet Hilton, worked steadily. They were pretty girls and not foolish. They worked burlesque as an "added attraction" and worked all over the country. When they worked a show, it meant one less dance routine for the chorus line. They did a pretty good act. They sang amazingly well, opening with "Side by Side," and they also sang "My Blue Heaven." Then they played ukuleles, saxophones, or clarinets, and ended with a nifty soft-shoe number. Their act lasted about twenty minutes. Daisy and Violet were pleasant and sociable girls, although it was hard for them. They had difficulty climbing long staircases. They were always nicely dressed, often wearing smashing, floor-length, silver lamé gowns."

Peter went on to say, "The Hilton sisters played many small towns on the circuits, mainly working two shows a night and sometimes a matinee. At one time, they were teamed with two identical male twins called "The Hartman Twins," who played piano accordions. They all traveled together with a stage manager and worked the clubs. The Hartman brothers played the entire show, which saved money. Each act did half an hour and no other musicians were needed. They all made a great deal of money."

I consider the photographs bought from Connie Fanslau's estate to be quite special, but as I continued my research, several other photos surfaced that made me believe these women were popular with fans and fellow performers.

Connie Fanslau Marquee.
PHOTO COURTESY OF: BURLESQUE HISTORICAL SOCIETY.

Daisy and Violet.
PHOTO COURTESY OF: DIANE DE LYS.

Daisy and Violet Hilton.
PHOTO COURTESY OF: BURLESQUE HISTORICAL SOCIETY.

Daisy and Violet Hilton.
PHOTO COURTESY OF: BURLESQUE HISTORICAL SOCIETY.

Daisy and Violet Hilton.

RIGHT:
Hilton Sisters Program.
PHOTO COURTESY OF:
BURLESQUE HISTORICAL SOCIETY.

BELOW:
Connie Fanslau Marquee.
PHOTO COURTESY OF:
BURLESQUE HISTORICAL SOCIETY.

April March
"The First Lady of Burlesque"

I first met April March after Carmela, "The Sophia Loren of Burlesque," gave me her address during the 1999 Las Vegas reunion. There were two burlesque dancers using the last name March: April March and June March.

April March was a sweet little girl born in 1935 in Oklahoma City. Her birth name was Velma Fern Worden. She appeared in an *Our Gang* comedy that was filmed in Oklahoma City when she was a ten-year-old, and that was when the show business bug first bit. April originally became involved in burlesque to pursue an acting career, and in the mid-1950s, Columbia Movie Studios approached her twice. They wanted to place her under contract and send her to acting school. Republic Studios also approached her to make a Western, but by then, April March, "The First Lady of Burlesque," loved working in burlesque so much, she turned both studios down.

As a child, Velma studied tap, ballet, and acrobatic dance. At the age of seventeen, she was hired as a copy girl for the *Daily Oklahoman*. Realizing this was not the job for her; she answered an ad, lied about her age, and went to work as a cigarette and flower girl at the Derby Club. Watching the dancers on stage and talking to people backstage, Velma decided she wanted to become a dancer with the show. Then, Barney Weinstein walked into the club one night, and he forever changed Velma's life. Weinstein and Mae, his wife, owned the Theatre Lounge in Dallas, Texas. Velma caught his eye and he convinced her to work for him as a dancer in his club. Barney not only gave Velma her first chance on stage as a dancer, but he also provided her stage name, "April March."

From 1952 to 1978, April had a long career in burlesque. From 1954, she performed as a feature in clubs, theatres, dinner theatre, and revues. She worked all over the United States, Canada, and in Mexico. Then in 1963, she headed off to perform in Manchester, England, but after only three months, she came home to the states, homesick for family and friends.

Immediately upon her return, she went to work for Harold Minsky, starring in two of his shows. April said that when she worked the first Minsky show, she spent a lot of her free time sitting in a coffee shop and playing gin rummy with the boys. During the second Minsky show, April chummed around with Joe E. Ross, who later went on to fame in the *Car 54* television series. In-between the Minsky shows, April worked six weeks for Ann Corio in, *This Was Burlesque.* She liked working with Ann, and during a press party thrown by Miss Corio for April, a magazine editor discovered that April was a talented golfer with a seven handicap. Because of that interview, she became the first female exotic dancer from burlesque to be given a full write-up in *Sports Illustrated.*

From 1956 to 1960, April was semi-retired from the burlesque stage, while she was married to a drugstore owner/pharmacist. During this time, she was Vice-President of the Women's Golf Association at the Tulsa Country Club.

In 1964, April signed a contract to appear in *Time Piece*, a film short made by Jim Henson and the Henson Studios. The nine-minute film went on to win a number of major awards within the film industry. It was a truly unique and amazing short film.

In 1982, a few short years after her retirement from burlesque, the Wayne, New Jersey Circus, Saints, and Sinners organization held a roast honoring April. The show benefited the American Cancer Society and was a big success.

Asked if she would become a striptease dancer and do it all over again, April responded, "No way, not today. Today it's not show business. If I could go back and do it in the days when it was fun, I would. I was always elegantly dressed, did a lot of teasing, and performed a good routine. Today they have everything off before they even come out on stage."

April opened her act with "I'll Remember April," and she also often used "Barefoot Countessa." Other songs used in her routines included "Man and a Woman," "Spellbound," "Harlem Nocturne," any "April" songs she could find, and music that was written especially for her. She closed her act with "Girl from Ipanema."

April loved working with Jimmy Mathews and Maxie Furman. Other favorite comics included Billy "Cheese N' Crackers" Hagen, Tommy "Moe" Raft, and Charlie Robinson. She liked them all because all the comics were very nice to her.

Like many others, April preferred working theatres to clubs. April had several favorite theatres and especially enjoyed working in St. Louis, Missouri, at the Garrick Theatre. Other favorites included the Gayety Theatre, in Washington, D.C., The Troc, in Philadelphia, and the Lyric Theatre, in Allentown, Pennsylvania. She also liked working at the Town Hall Theatre in Toledo, Ohio, for Rose La Rose.

Once, while April was performing in Florida, King Saud of Saudi Arabia became infatuated with her. After seeing her dance, he was so taken with her beauty and charm that he wanted to whisk her away, back to his kingdom. April said it was exciting to meet the King and to be transported in his limousine with all his bodyguards, but she politely declined his marriage offer.

Pilgrim Theatre marquee, Boston, Massachusetts.
PHOTO COURTESY OF: APRIL MARCH.

April March.
PHOTO COURTESY OF: APRIL MARCH.

April felt that most features in burlesque were not very friendly, but she always tried to be chummy with everyone. She remains active and loves animals, time with family and friends, traveling, and is a member of the Red Hat Society.

April explains, "My act was sexy, but dignified. My philosophy was to leave a little something to the imagination." When asked what the first thing "The First Lady of Burlesque" took off on stage, she replied, "A lady always removes her gloves first."

April March.
PHOTOS COURTESY OF: APRIL MARCH.

April March.
PHOTOS COURTESY OF: APRIL MARCH.

April March performing at the Piccadilly Club, in Miami Beach, Florida, 1966.
PHOTO COURTESY OF: APRIL MARCH.

April March performing at the Victory Theatre, in Toronto, Canada, 1964.
PHOTO COURTESY OF: APRIL MARCH.

Victory Theatre marquee advertising April March.
PHOTO COURTESY OF: APRIL MARCH.

April March.
PHOTO COURTESY OF:
APRIL MARCH.

April March and straight man Burt Gehan standing in front of the Pilgrim Theatre, Boston, Massachusetts, 1974.
PHOTO COURTESY OF: APRIL MARCH.

FROM LEFT TO RIGHT: **straight man Murray Briscoe, Harold Minsky, April March, and comic Charlie Robinson while working together during the 10 week run of the Minsky Show at Manor Hotel in Wildwood, New Jersey, 1964.**
PHOTO COURTESY OF: APRIL MARCH.

Ilka De Cava and April March admiring April's 12 foot likeness created to advertise the Minsky Show in Wildwood, New Jersey, 1964.
PHOTO COURTESY OF: APRIL MARCH.

Ann Corio and April March.
PHOTO COURTESY OF: APRIL MARCH.

April March, while appearing at the Town Hall Theatre for Rose La Rose.
PHOTO COURTESY OF: APRIL MARCH.

Rose La Rose and April March.
PHOTO COURTESY OF: APRIL MARCH.

Burlesque front advertising April March.
PHOTO COURTESY OF: APRIL MARCH.

April March

And the Shooting at Place Pigalle

A story I have heard from several people, including April March and Dixie Evans, revolved around a club shooting that happened on September 11, 1962, at The Place Pigalle at 215 22nd Street in Miami Beach. At 2:00 am that fateful morning, two men, Kun-Wha Yoo and Ray Allen Oglesby, walked into the club and changed the lives of many people. After inviting a young Korean woman to join them at their table for drinks, exotic dancer April March came out on stage and performed. A deafening burst of applause greeted her at the conclusion of her routine, just as another woman was invited to join the two men's table. Tony D'Arcy, a young baritone, was also invited to join their party. After her performance, April joined them, as well. Drinks and champagne were flowing freely, and when the $74 tab arrived, it was presented to Yoo. The Korean blew up, declaring that he had only ordered three drinks—not even the minimum of three drinks per person—and that was all he would pay for. He denied asking the girls, or anyone else, to join their table, and he denied responsibility for any champagne that was ordered. When the waiter insisted he pay, Yoo became violent. With their tab left unpaid, club steward Sal Hoffner and Tony D'Arcy physically evicted Yoo and Oglesby from the club.

Indignant, Yoo and Oglesby went back to their hotel room. While ignoring his friend's advice, Yoo loaded two handguns and returned to the club. Yoo's cab arrived back at the club at 3:50 am. D'Arcy, stepping outside for a breath of fresh air, was the first to see Yoo arrive and warned him not to go back inside. Yoo stepped toward the young singer, and with no warning, shot the man twice. D'Arcy screamed and fell. Dave Goodman, the seventy-two-year-old doorman, also tried to prevent Yoo from entering the club and was shot below the knees in both legs. Brandy Martin was performing on stage as the shots rang out. The music stopped and Sharon Sutton, billed as "The Upside Down Girl," jumped in front of April March to protect her, just as Yoo aimed his gun to fire off more shots. Sutton was shot point-blank, one bullet in her leg and another in her arm. Hoffner, watching from the kitchen doorway, threw a huge bongo drum at Yoo, throwing him off balance and knocking the gun from his hand. Earl Van, the show's emcee, rushed to Hoffner's aid. Goodman also stumbled in to assist, brandishing a prop machete from one of the acts.

Sharon Sutton, originally from East St. Louis, Illinois, lost her left leg, and in 1963, committed suicide. Tony D'Arcy died before the ambulances arrived. The doorman and a blonde contortionist dancer were also wounded. April March never again performed at The Place Pigalle. She immediately left to work the burlesque theatre circuit.

The club was closed down, but on September 19, manager Harry Ridge staged a grand reopening despite police orders to stay closed. It had also been recommended that the club's license not be renewed. The Miami Beach B-Girl patrol, a nightly patrol over five Miami Beach B-Girl Clubs, was also reactivated. The patrol had first begun when testimony before Congressional investigators about operations of such clubs brought Dade County bad publicity.

County Manager Irving McNayr stated, "The patrol will stay on now, this time, until we are dead certain the clubs have quit soliciting drinks." Yoo, who was also wanted for kidnapping and armed robbery in Georgia, was bound over to the grand jury on a first degree murder charge, and he eventually went to prison.

When asked why he committed the atrocity, Kun-Wha Yoo simply stated, "I just wanted to get even."

"Miss White Fury"

Born in October 1938, "Miss White Fury" was one of the offspring of an old-time Minneapolis radio couple, Rusty and Dusty Farnham. For years, the couple performed on WDGY Radio and even got married on the air. They worked in vaudeville, performing comedy routines, tap dancing, and singing, besides playing a variety of musical instruments. Baby Patti and her siblings grew up singing and dancing under their father's watchful eye. Under those circumstances, little else was on the youngster's mind other than dreaming of being a stage performer or a dancer.

At a very young age, Patti headed for Hollywood and went to work as a dance instructor. She met Coralie Jr., who became her agent. She was billed as "Miss White Fury and her Twin 44's." When working in clubs, she used the name Patti Kelly. She appeared on burlesque circuits as a feature attraction. Resplendent with platinum white hair, gorgeous white costumes, and twirling, large white tassels, she was in demand and an extremely popular performer. Patti knew how to dance and definitely had the figure for it. Those were the days of glamour, beautiful music, and live musicians. Patti considered comics and straight men the real stars of burlesque shows.

In one of the first letters I received from her, she wrote, "I twirled tassels—big tassels. You know, one this way and one that way. I worked the circuit as a feature. After my years in the theatres, I continued working in nightclubs."

Patti wrote long letters about her days in burlesque and memories of the people with whom she worked. "I consider myself a lucky person to have been involved in the days of burlesque, when shows were real shows. The theatres had first and second acts, openings, closings, finales, and costumes, and I made many friends I will never forget. Everyone was important, including the fabulous casts, the house people, the stage managers, theatre owners, and the orchestra players. Georgia Sothern was a wonderful, exciting feature to watch. Some of the gals in The Golden Days of Burlesque Historical Society were great talking women. They knew every scene and every comic. Gals like Grace Reed, Eileen Hubert, and Barbara Curtis. I never tired of watching the scenes and blackouts by such comic favorites as Irving Benson, Bert Carr, Maxie Furman, Ray Kolb, and Harry Conley."

"I had such a wonderful life on the road. Mostly good and fun things happened. A great deal of time was spent creating a new act with new costumes and props. Simon Sorr was my designer and one of the best. Publicity photos were very important, and Gene LaVerne, in Buffalo, New York, had a magic touch. I have really missed the friendships and the closeness I came to share with others in each and every show I worked. Believe me, there is no other feeling to compare. I think I can speak for all the people that stood on the burlesque stages."

Patti also recalled, "There was a time when many nightclubs featured class acts, and I had the opportunity to work some clubs like Marino's, in Portland, Oregon; The Stage Door, in Buffalo, New York, and The Hi-way Casino, in Fall River, Massachusetts. I was always treated like a real star. Dancers such as Taffey O'Neil were so beautiful. Every time I hear "Sophisticated Swing," I think of her. "Boots Malloy" (Sally Marr) and her son, Lenny Bruce were a blast. All of these people and many more, made up some of the greatest shows on earth!"

After retiring from burlesque, "Miss White Fury" became involved in ballroom dancing; she went on to become an instructor, and opened her own dance studio. Patti also owned restaurants, a tavern, retail shops, and a talent agency, yet every entertainment connection remained important to her. Being happy, healthy, and close with her family and friends is what matters most to her now.

"Why can't burlesque theatres' be revived," she asks, "instead of people thinking that topless, bottomless, table-dancing, pole-dancing, and lap-dancing is burlesque-related, or even stripping?" She is not alone in expressing these words and emotions. Many others feel the same way.

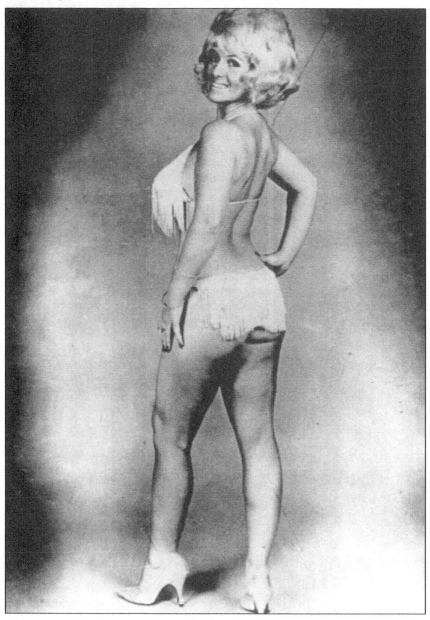

Miss White Fury, shortly before retirement.
PHOTO COURTESY OF: MISS WHITE FURY.

Miss White Fury.
PHOTO COURTESY OF:
MISS WHITE FURY.

Miss White Fury.
PHOTO COURTESY
OF: MISS WHITE
FURY.

Miss White Fury.
PHOTO COURTESY OF: MISS
WHITE FURY.

**Performing at the Lux
Theatre in Toronto,
Canada, 1964.**
PHOTO COURTESY OF:
MISS WHITE FURY.

White Fury, Sunny Dare, and Baby Doll, backstage at the Stage Door Club, in Buffalo, New York, around 1961.
PHOTO COURTESY OF: MISS WHITE FURY.

Victory Theatre Marquee in Toronto, Canada, 1964.
PHOTO COURTESY OF: MISS WHITE FURY.

Ray Kolb.
PHOTO COURTESY OF:
MISS WHITE FURY.

ABOVE AND
RIGHT:
**Miss White
Fury.**
PHOTOS
COURTESY
OF:
BURLESQUE
HISTORICAL
SOCIETY.

Miss White Fury.
PHOTO COURTESY OF: BURLESQUE HISTORICAL SOCIETY.

Sunny Dare
"The Girl with the Blue Hair"

Sunny Dare was a part of The Golden Days of Burlesque Historical Society since its inception, but I met her for the first time at our 2006 reunion. She was well-liked and respected among her fellow performers, so I asked her to write about her experiences in her own words:

"I've had "vagabond shoes" all my life, and being born on a carnival with a mom who played with snakes and a dad who broke horses made it easy to start somewhere in show business; for me it was burlesque. I loved to travel, and in 1950, I was in Detroit when I heard about a call for girls needed for the Sally Rand Show, which would tour the State Fair circuit. I got in touch with Sally, and she said they would be playing fair dates all the way from Detroit to Texas. She said they especially needed "Bally" girls. Sally explained that we would do no strips, but would just be outside posing. I thought, "*Great*." My food and all traveling expenses would be paid and I'd be getting a world of experience.

"My show business education took me around the globe, but unfortunately, it began with a rocky start. At the end of the fair Sally "stiffed" us. There I was in Texas with no money, no ticket home, and I didn't know a soul except the other girls, but I got lucky. Through an agent, I got a job at the Shriner's Club for one night—stripping! I really faked my way through that, but got enough money for a ticket home. I knew I wasn't finished in the business."

"A couple of weeks after returning home, I went back up to Detroit to the Gayety Burlesque Theatre and spoke with Frances Parks, the choreographer. She was great, and I started as a chorus girl right then and there. It was the beginning of a wonderful experience. A few months later, I was promoted to a co-feature. I met a lot of the other girls at that time in burlesque: Rose La Rose, Peaches, Georgia Sothern, Lois de Fee, Charmaine, Ann Arbor, Ricki Covette, and Patti Waggin. It was all a big thrill for me. Then, there were the comics and straight men: Al Anger, Scurvy Miller, Billy Hagen, Harry Conley, Looney Lewis, Art Watts, Erby Wallace, Herbie Barris, and so many others like Barbara Curtis, Joey Cowan, Earl Van, Al Murray, and Billy Ainsley."

"I loved the theatres. I never really cared about the money. I stood on the dark stage and heard a humming from the audience until it got quiet. Then, the announcer began. 'And now our feature attraction . . . Sunny Dare.' The curtains opened, the band played, and the spotlight hit me. It was glorious! It always made me feel like I was somebody special. The next twenty minutes were all mine. For a seventeen-year-old kid, who was already a big ham, I played it for all it was worth. Life was great."

"I played clubs a few times, and tried the carnies, but didn't like it. I really miss the life. Thank heaven for memories! I have a travel bug in me and would still be up there if it weren't for old father time. In the early days, I could see people's eyes when they heard what I did for a living. They used words like 'slut, stripper, party girl, and chippee.' The list goes on, but I never let it bother me. I knew what went on when the show was over. Backstage was like a big home; people were always cooking something on a small electric plate, and often babies were sleeping in the bottom drawer of our trunks with the whole crew baby-sitting. I never had children, but there's no way I can count how many times I cooked chicken or some other tasty morsel backstage for my little white poodle, Puddles, a very fitting name I might add. Every once in a while, I ran into another feature, but usually I'd finish my show, pack up, and be gone before the next act even appeared. Working all over the globe made it hard to see the other acts the other features were doing. In one of my routines, I had a large drum covered in silver cloth, and I did a lot of leg work. I made most of my own costumes. Every so often, I'd get Gene LaVerne to take new photos to go along with a new gown. Garbo was another great photographer, and Tony Midnite was a great costumer from Chicago. I photographed well—had blonde hair and a great smile. For a while, I went on a kick and changed my hair color to royal blue. That was really an attention getter!"

"I worked all the theatres, but like everyone else, we all had our favorites. I liked the Hudson Theatre in Union City, New Jersey, and also the theatre in Youngstown, Ohio. It was nice that everything, like travel arrangements, was taken care of for us. We'd close the show, pack the trunks early, and they were taken to the train and met in whatever city we were going to next. We slept on the train and woke up in another city, ready to go on with the show. I've traveled the whole globe, to the Dominican Republic in 1956 with a Minsky Review, to England in 1959, to Italy in 1960, to Canada in 1961, and to Japan in 1962."

"After all our traveling, my fourth and last husband and I landed in Florida. It was there where I saw a part of the business that made me wonder, "*Do I want to do that?*" The answer was a big, "No!" I realized I had better start looking for a new career. Burlesque as we knew it was gone. Theatres were no longer using live music for the dancers. There were no more beautiful chorus lines, comedians were fourth rate, and the girls were working so filthy that there was no way I wanted to be a part of that."

"So I bought an Arabic record, a set of Zils, which are finger cymbals, and proceeded to teach myself how to belly dance. Thank heaven I could dance. It was a perfect set up. I decided to go into nursing, a big step from my former job. I spent two years in school and looked forward to the day when I could perform my new profession on a full-time basis. I used to take my homework with me when I had a gig. I sat backstage working on my papers. Then when the time came, I went on stage, did my number, and then went home to a good night's sleep and another day of schooling. I worked the Fontainebleau Hotel, the largest hotel on Miami Beach, and met so many wonderful people willing to help in my time of need."

"It all fell into place, and things went so well that I decided to increase my degrees while I was still young enough. So for the next two years, I went for more training and became a nurse anesthetist. My burlesque days were some of the best years of my life and will always be a part of me. Turn up the lights, start the music, and there I am—Sunny Dare, a Burlesque Queen!"

While going through Sunny's scrapbooks, I uncovered that Sunny began working in the Sally Rand Carnival Show in September 1950. Her first show was in Nashville, Tennessee. During October 7-22, they played the Texas State Fair, apparently at a time when the cast was not paid for their work. In January 1951, Sunny was appearing in her first chorus line at the Gayety Theatre in Detroit. On April 28, 1951, an article titled "Burlesque Bits" in the *Toledo Blade* reported: "Bobbie Rogers, (Sunny) a new strip promoted by Arthur Clamage, opened at the Gayety in Toledo for a tour of the Midwest Circuit." By December 1951, her stage name had been changed to "Sunny Dare," and she was being called "a shapely dance stylist" by newspaper columnists. She had already become a feature attraction. Initially, she told me she wanted to use the stage name "Sunny Day," but it was already being used by another dancer.

Her appearances were as numerous as the people with whom she worked with. In 1952, Sunny was billed as "The Girl with the Blue Hair;" and to quote a newspaper clipping, "In her dances she displays the grace of a jungle tiger cat." She was a popular performer. Various newspapers across the country included the following quotes about Sunny Dare:

"SHE DARES TO BE DIFFERENT,"
"THRILL TO HER ACROBATIC DANCING,"
"THE BRIGHT SIDE OF BURLESQUE,"
"THE MOST DARING GIRL IN TOWN,"
"DARES TO BE SENSATIONAL,"
"HOLLYWOOD SHOW GIRL,"
"THE GIRL WITH THE MILLION DOLLAR LEGS,"
"THE ESQUIRE GIRL,"
"THE TORRID TIGER,"
"THE INTERNATIONAL FIREBALL,"
"MISS FIFTH AVENUE,"
"SUNNY (DON'T YOU) DARE."

In 1959, in her column, "A Look at Burlesque with Rita Atlanta," Rita Atlanta wrote, "She likes to travel, does this Sunny Dare, and she makes the most of her opportunities, which lately have been many. It is difficult to tell just how Sunny got her name, as it could have been either because of her head of flaming red hair or her cheerful and sunny disposition. But however she got it, it fits. Sunny has been a stripper for nine years and her act consists of more than just shedding her clothes to music. Sunny combines acrobatic and Cuban dances with her stripping, and the audiences love every minute of it, which just goes to prove that burlesque fans like some dancing with their favorite art."

Rita went on to write, "Sunny is not only well known on the burlesque circuit, but has played in night clubs in most parts of the country as well as in England, Italy, Dominican Republic, and Tokyo."

In 1962, she began performing as a belly dancer up and down the East coast until she returned to school in Florida to study nursing. As "Nejma," she was billed as "King Farouk's Favorite Dancer," "Queen of the Harem," and "The Turkish Delight."

Sunny had so many routines and stage personas that no one knew what to expect when they saw her perform. I am glad I finally got to meet her at our 2006 reunion. She was one-of-a-kind in burlesque and a friend to all, especially four-legged critters. On August 8, 2008, Sunny Dare passed away, and she is missed by many.

Sally Rand Revue of 1950, including cast and stage hands.
Photo courtesy of: Sunny Dare.

LEFT:
Photo signed to Bobby from Sally Rand; Dallas, Texas, October 1950.
PHOTO COURTESY OF: SUNNY DARE.

BELOW LEFT:
Photo taken while performing under the name of Bobbie Rogers.
PHOTO COURTESY OF: SUNNY DARE.

BELOW RIGHT:
Sunny Dare.
PHOTO COURTESY OF: SUNNY DARE.

After retiring as Sunny Dare and performing as Nejma.
PHOTO COURTESY OF: SUNNY DARE.

Nejma.
PHOTO COURTESY OF: SUNNY DARE.

Snapshot of Sally Rand Revue; Nashville, Tennessee, 1950.
PHOTO COURTESY OF: SUNNY DARE.

1955, Washington D.C. advertisement.
PHOTO COURTESY OF: SUNNY DARE.

Sunny Dare.
PHOTO COURTESY OF: SUNNY DARE.

Bobbie Rogers with Sally Rand's fans; Nashville, Tennessee, September 1950.
PHOTO COURTESY OF: SUNNY DARE.

Bobbie Rogers relaxing between shows while performing with the Sally Rand Revue in Nashville, Tennessee, in 1950.
PHOTO COURTESY OF: SUNNY DARE.

Frances Parks; choreographer at the Gayety Theatre in Detroit, Michigan, in 1951.
PHOTO COURTESY OF: SUNNY DARE.

Sunny Dare.
PHOTO COURTESY OF: SUNNY DARE.

Hudson Theatre program; Union City, New Jersey, September 1954.
PHOTO COURTESY OF: SUNNY DARE.

Sunny Dare.
PHOTO COURTESY OF: SUNNY DARE.

Sunny Dare.
PHOTO COURTESY OF: SUNNY DARE.

Sunny Dare; Detroit, Michigan in 1959.
PHOTO COURTESY OF: SUNNY DARE.

Marquee photos, from when Sunny appeared in Canada.
PHOTO COURTESY OF: SUNNY DARE.

Backstage snapshots of the cast from Sunny's first Road Show including: Rita Ravell, Sunny, Norma Jean Watson, Art Watts, Erby Wallace, and Nat Mercy.
PHOTO COURTESY OF: SUNNY DARE.

Advertisement for Sunny's first Road Show at the Gayety Theatre in Dayton, Ohio, on September 12, 1952.
PHOTO COURTESY OF: SUNNY DARE.

Blaze Fury

"**B**laze Fury" was a burlesque performer I never had the opportunity to communicate with, although I was close to finding her when I learned of her death. However, several members of the Burlesque Historical Society have told me she had a long history on the burlesque stage and was highly-respected among performers and stagehands alike.

Blaze was born Lucia Parks, the third generation of her family to work in show business. Her mother, Frances Parks, had worked in silent films before becoming a dancer in burlesque. Her grandmother, Opal Parks Gilmore, had been a trapeze artist working with a circus. Her father was a respected musician.

In the late 1940s, Lucia dropped out of high school while in the eleventh grade, and she went to work in her mother's chorus line at the Gayety Theatre in Detroit. Before long, she worked her way up to become a house-strip, and for many years, went on to feature in road shows on the burlesque circuit. Then, tragedy struck and Lucia developed tuberculosis. The late Peter Thomas mentioned in a letter how the young dancer went to the Variety Club's Sanitarium in Saranac Lake, New York, to regain her health. After gaining some weight, new gowns were made, and then she returned to the circuit as "Blaze Fury, The Human Heat Wave." Her costumes were all hand-made by her mother and grandmother. If any costume repairs were needed while she worked in shows across the country, she made them herself. Lucia traveled everywhere with her sewing machine.

Blaze was a strong and determined woman. In a 1953 *Cavalcade of Burlesque* magazine interview, she stated, "It's everybody's favorite indoor pastime to psychoanalyze the burlesque dancer. When are people going to realize that we're in burlesque because we like show business and like to dance? Half the girls have mothers or grand-mothers who have been in show business. It runs in families, like musical talent. It's also traditional to scoff when you read that a burlesque girl supports a family, attends opera, and reads good books, but that's exactly the truth. We have nothing to be ashamed of. We're proud of our art and our morals are as high as career girls anywhere. In fact, I've heard more vulgar talk among a group of stenographers than I've heard around a dressing room."

After working as a dancer in burlesque for nearly thirty years, Blaze retired in 1978 at the age of fifty. Even before hanging up her g-string, she knew that the era of creativity with striptease as an art form was coming to an end. Like many other dancers from burlesque, she complained about too much nudity in the clubs. Blaze never even considered working in the nude and always wore a fully-beaded and exaggerated g-string, along with full pasties. She once said, "I always had more on when I finished my act than what they wear on the beach today. These girls today are just naked ladies. They do nothing with nothing on."

Blaze served as a National Executive Board Member of the American Guild of Variety Artists, and in 1996, she retired as the business agent for Local 786 of the International Alliance of Theatrical Stage Employees. She was also an active volunteer with the Muscular Dystrophy Association. Throughout her career, her billing read "Blaze Fury, often imitated, but never equalized." She was always highly-respected by all who knew and worked with her. Blaze Fury was the widow of comic Tommy Timlin. She was a breast cancer survivor, but on May 28, 1997, she died of heart failure in Warren, Michigan.

Photo collage of Lucia Parks.

Blaze Fury.
PHOTO COURTESY OF: BURLESQUE HISTORICAL SOCIETY.

LEFT:
Frances Parks, mother of Lucia Parks, also known as Blaze Fury.
PHOTO COURTESY OF: LEE STUART.

BELOW:
Frances Parks.
PHOTO COURTESY OF: LEE STUART.

Blaze Fury.
PHOTOS COURTESY OF:
BURLESQUE HISTORICAL
SOCIETY.

Georgia Sothern

Georgia was born Hazel Anderson in Dungannon, Georgia. Shortly after her birth, her father abandoned the family. Her mother hammered out a meager living for herself and her young daughter by selling short stories to women's magazines, writing under the name Corey Estelle. Hazel's uncle worked as an actor with a stock company in Atlanta. When the small child performing with his company became too ill to go on stage, he suggested his four-year-old niece for the role.

For the next nine years, Hazel and her uncle toured the vaudeville circuits with her mother in tow. Hazel grew up on stage, performing in dramas and musicals as an acrobat, toe dancer, singer, and actress.

In 1931, when vaudeville was on its last legs, Hazel was in a show that folded and stranded them in Philadelphia. Upon hearing that the Bijou Theatre was hiring young girls, she went for an audition, but she had no idea that the Bijou Theatre was a house of burlesque. All the young woman knew about burlesque was that it embarrassed her mother whenever the subject came up. The $50 a week salary she was offered was too tempting to refuse. She needed work and accepted the job. When asked for her name, Hazel replied, "Georgia Sothern." She planned on working in burlesque for only a few weeks before returning to vaudeville.

Georgia remembered, "I didn't know a damn thing about what I was supposed to do, other than dance and take my clothes off. I still don't know what I did out there, but it brought the house down. I was quite mature for thirteen and they liked me—and I liked them right back. The stripping part never bothered me for a minute. And my mother was so happy about the $50 she wasn't even embarrassed."

After only two short months, Georgia Sothern became a star performer on the burlesque stage, first appearing at the Troc in Philadelphia. She was signed by Minsky's to headline at their Republic Theatre on 42nd Street in New York City. During the 1930s and 1940s, when she was not at Minsky's, Georgia got top billing at nearly every major burlesque theatre in the country, usually earning $3,500 a week. Occasionally, she played state fairs that paid her up to $5,000 a day, but she never once performed on a burlesque stage in Atlanta, Georgia.

In 1942, Georgia appeared at the Music Box Theatre in New York City in the Broadway Revue, *Star and Garter*, which was produced by Michael Todd and starred Gypsy Rose Lee and Bobby Clark. The show, promoted as so-called legitimate burlesque, opened to packed houses just three months after Mayor La Guardia and Paul Moss put New York City burlesque theatres totally out of business by refusing to renew their licenses. For many months, she continued working in this revue at the Blackstone Theatre, in Chicago.

In 1943, Georgia performed in *The Naked Genius*, a play written by Gypsy Rose Lee, produced by Michael Todd, and starring Joan Blondell. Georgia increasingly made more nightclub appearances with the Ritz Brothers or various name bands. From the late 1940s through the 1950s, she appeared in summer stock productions, including highly-rated performances in *Personal Appearances, Separate Rooms*, and *Burlesque*. She continued to perform in burlesque as late as 1967, but only for the top houses that could afford her salary. Those became increasingly rare. Georgia also appeared in some television roles.

Georgia loved burlesque and the people involved in the business. Later in life, she said, "Burlesque quit me. I never would have left the business if it hadn't changed so much. It got so nobody cared anymore."

Georgia Sothern's billing stated she was "Perpetual Motion" and "Dynamite." Those who knew her and saw her perform said that her energetic dancing accounted for her fame. Georgia opened her act with "Georgia on my Mind," and closed it with "Tiger Rag," which was played in the fastest tempo possible. She tore around the stage like a human dynamo. In his review of, *Star and Garter* for the *New York Times*, Brooks Atkinson called Georgia Sothern "unpretentiously hot stuff."

In the early 1950s, *Focus Magazine* ran a survey and calculated the top ten women who could stop traffic faster than a New York City cop. Georgia Sothern found her name on that list. The others included Carmen Amaya, Denise Darcel, Marlene Dietrich, Katherine Dunham, Ava Gardner, Anna Magnani, Edith Piaf, Jane Russell, and Kathleen Winsor.

Fellow strippers Gypsy Rose Lee and Mildred "Peaches" Strange were Georgia's closest friends. In the 1930s, she was married very briefly to Les Sponsler. Even though she always claimed her one great love was show business, in 1955 she eventually married a second time to attorney John J. Diamond. In 1972, her autobiography, *Georgia: My Life in Burlesque*, was published and edited by her close friend, Mickey Spillane.

Exotic dancer Jewel Sothern was generally believed to be Georgia's sister. In March 1999, Margie Hart wrote me a letter stating, "Georgia died a few years ago from cancer." Georgia was sixty-eight years old when she passed away on October 14, 1981, at Memorial Sloan-Kettering Hospital in New York.

Georgia Sothern on stage, 1947.
PHOTO COURTESY OF: BURLESQUE HISTORICAL SOCIETY.

Jewel Sothern.

**Georgia
Sothern.**

Georgia Sothern relaxing at home, 1948.
PHOTO COURTESY OF: BURLESQUE HISTORICAL SOCIETY.

Marquee advertising Georgia Sothern—and to verify this is HOW she spelled her name.
PHOTO COURTESY OF: PAT ELLIOTTMINSKY/BURLESQUE HISTORICAL SOCIETY.

Georgia Sothern.
PHOTO COURTESY OF:
BURLESQUE HISTORICAL
SOCIETY.

**Georgia
Sothern.**
PHOTO
COURTESY OF:
BURLESQUE
HISTORICAL
SOCIETY.

School for Strippers

In 1951, the first school to train young, hopeful exotic dancers opened its doors in Los Angeles. Classes were held backstage at the New Follies Theatre. Lillian Hunt not only ran the school, but she also produced the burlesque shows. She was more than qualified, having been involved in burlesque most of her life. Plus, comic Leon De Voe, her husband, was on hand to help. The classes were held mornings and afternoons for five hours a day, when the stage was not occupied by a show. Most of the students were beginners; however Lillian also offered a "refresher course," which was attended by some older dancers already performing in burlesque. At the school for strippers, new students were taught the tricks to the trade, including a variety of dance steps, theatrical make-up, disrobing techniques, posture, stage presence, and how to sew and create costumes.

In those years, burlesque was a profession; it played a major role in show business. Exotic dancers, just as any other trade, had skills to be learned. Lillian taught those girls how to dance and disrobe on stage without appearing awkward and self-conscious. A good striptease dancer walked with her whole body, not just her legs, and the young women learned how to walk correctly.

The young exotic dancers all had beauty and a shapely figure, but Lillian realized that they required training to be a success in burlesque, and she provided the know-how. She emphasized routines that helped the dancers develop their own stage personalities. Costumes, make-up, dancing, and movements were tailored to each student.

Rex Huntington
"Costume Designer Extraordinaire"

Once upon a time, burlesque shows were filled with comics and straight men, talking women, chorus lines, and house-singers. The exotic queens of the burlesque stage wore spectacular costumes of ornate satin and rhinestones, all the while retaining an air of glamour and mystery. During those years, many audience members did not simply attend burlesque shows to see the bodies; they came to see the beautiful gowns and magnificent costumes created by designers such as Rex Huntington.

Rex was born in Richmond, Indiana. In the late 1920s, he began his show business career as a dancer in vaudeville. Upon his first glimpse into a wardrobe shop filled with satin, sequins, feathers, and rhinestones, he realized his destiny. Rex continued to dance, but in his spare time, he gradually built a reputation as a costume designer.

In 1948, he quit dancing altogether and began creating costumes full-time. During the mid-1950s, he teamed with Robert Lockwood in Chicago. They moved east and set up shop in New Jersey. Due to the amount of work they did for the Hudson Theatre, one of the top burlesque houses in the country, Huntington and Lockwood soon became the most sought after costumers in burlesque, with the biggest and best names in burlesque beating a path to their door. Rex designed the costumes, and both he and Robert sewed them.

For more than fifty years, Rex designed wardrobe for more than 300 performers. He chose between satin or lace, rhinestones or sequins, feathers or beads, and he wove them into spectacular costumes. Dancers paid anywhere from a few hundred to a few thousand dollars for his creations. Just some of the exotic dancers

Rex made costumes for included Zorita, Joan Torino, Dixie Evans, Lois de Fee, Georgia Sothern, Irma the Body, Trudine the Shimmy Queen, Rose La Rose, Lotus DuBois, Peaches, and Tempest Storm. Whereas vaudeville performers often wore the same costumes over and over again, burlesque performers could not always get away with that. Often, a dancer was expected to wear a dazzling new gown at every performance. Rex was popular because he made the women look good.

In later years, Huntington and Lockwood worked out of a studio created on the top floor of their Weehawken, New Jersey home. During the late 1960s and 1970s, their sewing machines began growing silent as burlesque was dying a slow death. The demand for satin panels and elaborate rhinestone striptease costumes had all but disappeared. Their studio became overcrowded with dress dummies, mannequin heads, and old sewing machines that were no longer used. Closets were full of spools of sequins, feathers, and long strings of plastic beads, while the tables were heaped with finished and unfinished gowns and materials. In 1983, Robert Lockwood died.

After Lockwood's death, Huntington only worked occasionally as a favor for old friends. In January 1992, Rex had hip replacement surgery, but shortly thereafter, he was up and dancing again. His mind remained clear and sharp, and he often entertained friends and visitors at great length with stories of show business life. On September 13, 1992, Rex Huntington died of a heart attack at the age of eighty-five.

Even though the glamorous and ornate theatrical palaces have nearly all been stripped of their glory and destroyed, Rex Huntington can never be stripped of his title as "Costume Designer Extraordinaire."

Lois de Fee.
PHOTO COURTESY OF:
BURLESQUE HISTORICAL
SOCIETY.

Georgia Sothern.
PHOTO COURTESY OF: JONI
TAYLOR.

Irma the Body.
PHOTO COURTESY
OF: JONI TAYLOR.

Irma the Body.
PHOTO COURTESY
OF: BURLESQUE
HISTORICAL
SOCIETY.

Rose La Rose.
Photos courtesy of: Burlesque Historical Society.

Trudine.
Photo courtesy of: Burlesque Historical Society.

Tempest Storm.
Photo courtesy of: Lady Midnight.

Irving Benson

From the time that young Irving could walk and talk, he was destined for a life in show business. At the age of eleven, he won his first amateur dancing contest. He worked as an actor until he was twenty-one-years old, and then he set foot on his first burlesque stage. He soon became one of the youngest featured comics to ever work in burlesque.

Over the years, he worked nightclubs and vaudeville, but he always returned to burlesque, his first love. His experience led to an occasional role in a Broadway show, including the part of Benny Southstreet in *Guys and Dolls*.

Irving wrote, "People tend to forget that two-a-day burlesque shows were the forerunner of what later became Broadway musicals. Before that, they only did dramatic shows. Shortly after the turn of the century, they saw what the Minsky's were doing. A house singer sang in each of the chorus numbers. The size of a show determined whether two straight men and two or three comics were used. In later years, very few shows had three comics. Some burlesque shows had an act—sometimes a vaudeville act or a specialty number—that they inserted into the show. We had to be able to do everything in those days: sing, dance, act, and do comedy. Burlesque shows were wonderful entertainment."

Irving auditioned for *The Milton Berle Show* on television. Berle and Bill Dana selected Irving over 200 other comics to play Berle's Man in the Box—Sidney Schpritzer. Besides appearing as a regular on Berle's television show, Irving worked on the *Vaudeville* television special with Berle and also appeared on five *Hollywood Palace* shows when Berle served as the host. For many years, they maintained a working friendship. As late as 1997, Irving and Milton toured together in a show in Florida.

Irving has also appeared on other television shows including *The Merv Griffin Show, Happy Days, Switch,* Alan King's special, *Comedy is King,* and a Joan Rivers special—just to name a few. He has also worked in television commercials.

While appearing at a nightclub in New York, Irving was seen by Johnny Carson. As long as Carson was host of *The Tonight Show,* Irving was a frequent guest. During his many appearances on the show, Johnny played straight man for Irving, which was one of the highest compliments that can be paid to a comedian by a fellow comedian.

Irving was known as a "comedian's comedian," and he worked as top banana all over the country. He has worked in Las Vegas at many hotels including The Dunes, New Frontier, Sahara, Silver Slipper, Union Plaza, Thunderbird, and the Aladdin. He also worked in *Minsky's Burlesque* at the Hacienda Hotel, and was Harold's principal comic for more than thirty years.

Irving remembered a few of the burlesque performers he worked with over the years. About Herbie Barris, he said, "Herbie started out early in his career as a singer and straight man, but along the way, he turned to comedy. He was a better straight man, but he continued to do comedy for years until he passed away. We worked together for a long time. He worked as the second comic."

About Myrna Dean, he said, "Wow! She worked with me for the first time, at the Republic Theatre on 42nd Street. We also worked on a road show together. Her mother used to travel with Myrna and always had a little bottle of gin in her purse. The old lady used to say it made her relax and kept her warm, if the weather got cold. She would have a little nip from time to time. Sometimes she got so relaxed she couldn't move. Myrna, at that time, was married to a comic named Slats Taylor. Slats and I first worked together at the Republic Theatre on 42nd Street in New York, around 1937. Myrna Dean was a good old gal."

About June March, he said, "June passed away in Atlantic City, in 1995. She was another beauty who died of cancer. She seemed fine the last time I saw her."

"Danny Morton was always a handsome guy, even when we first met in 1937 and were kids together in burlesque. I replaced him at the People's Theatre on the Bowery in New York as a singer, before they had an opening for me as a comic. Mickey Dennis was a little chorus girl with us. They got married young, as did my wife and I."

Irving recalled Taffey O'Neil. "What a lovely lady! She is one of my all-time favorite people I have ever met in show business. A real lady! No matter how many years pass, I'd know her anywhere. She will always have that same sweet face."

As for Diane Raye, he reminisced about his first job in Toronto, Canada. "It was at the Casino Theatre, and our feature was Diane Raye. She was eighteen or nineteen years old and had just come back from England, where she was a big hit. She was one of the loveliest women I ever saw. She looked just like Vivien Leigh—a real beauty."

"After receiving your letter telling me about Lili St. Cyr passing away, all I can say is, 'There went a great lady.' We were very friendly and had known each other a long time. Her sister, Dardy Orlando, and I go way back, even before she married Harold Minsky. I was Harold's principal comic for over thirty years. I was there when their daughter was born. Yet, I knew Dardy for forty years and never knew her real name."

Irving thought back to Diana Van Dyne. "What a nice shock it was to hear that you found Diana Van Dyne. This is, without a doubt, one of the nicest ladies it was ever my good fortune to work with. She exhibited such class. We worked together, a long time, at the Rialto Theatre in Chicago. We were in stock together. This girl was a great dancer in the class of Mimi Reed and she had such a wonderful sense of humor."

Irving worked with so many people over his long career in burlesque that it is hard to mention them all. Others included Lou Ascol, Al Baker, Sr., Bonnie Boyia, Charmaine, Ann Corio, Charlie Crafts, Barbara Curtis, Vicki "Babe" Davis, Lois de Fee, Carrie Finnell, Pat "Amber" Halliday, Margie Hart, Danny Jacobs, Sunny Knight, Beverly Lane, Louise Laurie, Jess Mack, Jimmy Mathews, Claude Mathis, Howard Montgomery, Mimi Reed, Dian Rowland, Sheila Ryan, Stunning Smith, and Georgia Sothern.

In May 1998, I received a letter from Irving that was written with great emotion. The letter was dated May 15, 1998, and he wrote, "Today is a sad day, the day that Frank Sinatra died. I first worked with him around 1940 when he had just joined the Dorsey Band. It was a Sunday concert at the Arena in New Haven, Connecticut. He was the greatest and there will never be another one like him."

Irving, an elf-like comedian, proved to the entire entertainment industry that the old adage, "big talent comes in a small package," was true. Whether he was working burlesque, Broadway, television, hotels, or nightclubs, he is a man of many talents.

Irving Benson.
AUTHORS COLLECTION.

Burlesque comics Joey Cowan and Irving Benson.
PHOTO COURTESY OF: IRVING BENSON.

Irving Benson in front of the Minsky marquee at the Thunderbird Hotel, in Las Vegas, Nevada, 1973.
PHOTO COURTESY OF: IRVING BENSON.

Irving Benson.

Backstage at the El Rancho in Las Vegas, from left to right: Irving Benson, Jessica James, Eddie Lynch and Jack Mann.
PHOTO COURTESY OF: PAT ELLIOTT MINSKY/BURLESQUE HISTORICAL SOCIETY.

Charlie Crafts.
PHOTO COURTESY
OF: BURLESQUE
HISTORICAL
SOCIETY.

**Pat "Amber"
Halliday,
1954.**
PHOTO
COURTESY
OF: THE
FASCINATING
JENNIFER.

Lili St. Cyr.
PHOTO COURTESY OF: PAT ELLIOTT MINSKY/BURLESQUE HISTORICAL SOCIETY.

Danny Morton.
PHOTO COURTESY OF: LEE STUART.

Louise Laurie.
PHOTO COURTESY OF: IRVING
BENSON.

Mickie Dennis.
AUTHORS COLLECTION.

Jess Mack.
Photo courtesy of: Al Baker Jr.

Myrna Dean.
Photo courtesy of:
Lee Stuart.

Monkey Kirkland

On July 14, 1909, James Orbry Monroe Kirkland was born into a show business family in Dallas, Texas. His mother, a half-Cherokee Indian, was a variety performer that was noted for her beauty and grace as an actress and dancer. His father, a man of Scottish/Irish descent, was blackface vaudeville comedian Benny "Beans" Kirkland.

Young James's first known stage role was at the age of twelve as a chorus girl in one of his father's shows. From what has been said of this performance, no one apparently knew he was a boy. With long hair, he looked like a girl, and he was a good dancer.

In 1929 when James starred in a production of *Charley's Aunt*, he changed his name to Monroe James Kirkland. The following year, he met Josephine Field, a young actress from an old show business family. In 1931, the young couple married. Soon after, the Kirkland clan began performing in tent shows. These shows included singing, dance routines, comedy bits, and variety acts, along with some serious dramas including *Uncle Tom's Cabin*. His entire family got into the act.

In 1933 the Kirkland's first child, a son, died during childbirth. In 1934, Josephine, backstage between acts, had barely finished her number in the first show when a call went out, "Is there a doctor in the house?" Benita, their daughter, was born prematurely. The doctor wrapped her in a blanket and left, not telling anyone he was rushing the tiny infant to a nearby convent. The nuns literally willed life into baby Benita, and they only returned her when they felt certain she would survive.

Whenever they were on stage, the Kirkland's fashioned a snug bed of soft, folded blankets in a theatrical trunk near the wings and placed their baby daughter safely there. Benita made her acting debut at six weeks of age, when she was carried on stage by a character in *Uncle Tom's Cabin*. Though their baby was born in Iola, Kansas, her birth was later filed in Texas. Their family members were all Texans on her father's side, and he wanted his first-born daughter to have a Texas birth certificate. In 1935, another son died in childbirth, and then Monkey and Josephine's marriage fell apart. They divorced, and Josephine left show business.

Monroe, affectionately called "Monkey," briefly performed in vaudeville, before turning to the burlesque stage full-time. As a top banana, he became popular with the crowds and traveled the circuits from coast to coast, billed as "Monkey Kirkland." Some time in the 1940s, he married a dancer named Jean. She was deaf and performed by feeling the vibrations from the music. They had a baby girl, but that marriage also did not survive.

Monkey was a handsome man, who was quite appealing to women when he was not dressed as a comic. He worked in shows with top feature dancers such as Zorita, Rose La Rose, Tempest Storm, Blaze Fury, Irma the Body, Blaze Starr, and many others. He married Kay Drew, a headliner, and together, they had three children—two daughters and a son.

In the early 1950s, Monkey opened a nightclub in Phoenix, Arizona, called the Lei Lani Club. Not only did Monkey have a natural flare for comedy, but he also painted, wrote, designed, and created terrific wardrobe. When one of the exotic dancers in his show accidentally ripped her gown before going on stage, Monkey draped some beautiful silk jersey material on her, pinned it at a few strategic points, and she looked like she had on a gown that cost a million bucks. All she had to do now was pull out a few pins in time with the music and her entire gown fell off.

After closing the Lei Lani, Monkey opened another club called Collette's, which was also in Phoenix. Everyone liked working for Kirkland, so his entire crew stayed with him. During the 1955 summer, Monkey, Kay, and their kids lived in a mobile home behind the club. Benita came to work for him as a dancer. Benita continued working for her father until November, when she moved to Los

Angeles and began working at the Follies Theatre as "Lady Midnight."
After four years as a regular at the theatre, she began working in
clubs and on the burlesque circuit.

In the late 1950s, Monkey and Kay separated and divorced. In
1960, Monkey went back to working the burlesque circuits, even
appearing at the Playboy Club in Chicago. He spent decades on the
road, working various theatres and clubs, and always staying in
touch with Benita. Over time, they grew close and became good
friends.

In 1969, Benita was in a horrendous car accident that nearly
ended her life. Monkey visited her while she was in intensive care
in the hospital, but it was only later that she even knew her father
was there. She spent the following five years in a wheelchair,
learning how to survive a different type of lifestyle than she was
used too.

Monkey continued working as often as possible, most notably in
1972 as a headliner at the Circus Circus Hotel and Casino in Las
Vegas. He still maintained a home in Texas. Then in April 1982,
Benita received a call from the Garza Funeral Home in Houston,
Texas, telling her of her father's accidental death. Monkey had been
driving through an intersection, when a sudden electrical fire burst
from under the dashboard of his car. Panicked, he made the
mistake of stopping to swat at the fire, not realizing he was in the
middle of the intersection. He was hit directly on the driver's side
by an oncoming vehicle. Monkey was airlifted to the hospital,
but he did not survive. The accident was a sad ending for a true,
old-time trooper from the golden days of burlesque, and his death
ended an era of laughter.

Monroe James Kirkland.
PHOTO COURTESY OF: LADY MIDNIGHT.

A Young "Monkey," age 25.
PHOTO COURTESY OF: LADY MIDNIGHT.

Lei Lani, Monkey's Club.
PHOTO COURTESY OF: LADY MIDNIGHT.

Monkey and the Lei Lani Lovelies.
PHOTO COURTESY OF: LADY MIDNIGHT.

Gayety show cast, Monkey 3rd from left.
PHOTO COURTESY OF: LADY MIDNIGHT.

Ralph Clifford and Monkey Kirkland.
PHOTO COURTESY OF: LADY MIDNIGHT.

Lady Midnight.
PHOTO COURTESY OF: LADY MIDNIGHT.

Kay Drew.
PHOTO COURTESY OF: LADY MIDNIGHT.

Kay Drew.
PHOTO COURTESY OF: LORRAINE LEE.

Dick Richards
"The Comic"

Born Richard Gluck on Staten Island, New York, Dick was the son of a millinery designer and a Cornell University Engineering Professor. When Richard was small, his father began losing his eyesight, so he joined relatives in a shoe business. Dick was the youngest of three children and the only son. From the age of eight, Dick studied piano and won a scholarship to the Julliard School of Music, where he studied for two years. However, formal education ended abruptly when Dick signed on as a band member on a cruise ship to South America. After being offered the job as the pianist, he found out performers were making $25 a week compared to his $12 a week playing the piano. He abruptly decided to change professions.

When Dick returned to the United States, he went to work on the Borscht Belt, the old hotel circuit in the Catskills, and he prepared for a career in comedy. After several months, he auditioned at the Eltinge Theatre on 42nd Street in New York and got the job.

After a few days, the theatre manager approached Dick. "Why don't you stutter anymore, like you did at the audition?"

Dick simply replied, "I don't stutter. I was just very nervous."

The manager told Dick to put the stutter back into his act, which he did, until the manager stopped paying such close attention to the show.

"At the time, I figured I'd only be in burlesque for a couple of years," he recalled. "Burlesque was still a stepping-stone to legitimate theatre, the movies, and everything in-between. I thought I'd hang around for a couple of years and just look at the girls."

Dick Richards certainly saw a lot of girls. Over the years, he watched as the dancers virtually drove the comics out of a business that originally revolved around comedy. As burlesque evolved, audiences wanted to see more of the dancers and less of a show. Living normal lives when they were not on the road, many dancers read, played cards, or knitted backstage between acts. They put themselves or husbands through college on their show business incomes.

Harold Minsky, who entered the business in 1933, once said, "I just think that you get more people turned on by teasing them than by coming out and showing them everything you've got. We were entertaining the working guy. Rich people had their Ziegfeld Follies, and the working guy had burlesque, where he could go see a show for 50¢ or 75¢. At the height of burlesque, our family owned seventeen theatres, and most were on the East coast."

Harold and Dick both believed that theatre owner's greed was a principal cause of burlesque's decline and fall. Seeking more profits, the owners began to pare down the shows and reduce the number of comics, straight men, chorus girls, and musicians. Then, they paid strippers higher and higher salaries.

Minsky said, "They took the feed away from the horse, until one day the horse died."

Dick recalled watching the horse die in New York City, while playing the last shows in Minsky's Gayety Theatre. "The operators of several burlesque houses on 42nd Street had become so competitive that they put up pictures of their strippers on the street, ignoring the growing resentment of the congregation of a nearby church."

Abbott and Costello's success inspired Dick. "The material they used was all the traditional stuff," he said. "They didn't have any writers, just John Grant, a good rewrite man. John took the old burlesque skits and made them suitable for the movies. That's why a lot of comedians, like me, thought of burlesque as a stepping-stone."

Dick worked regularly for Harold Minsky, but his performances were not limited to the burlesque stage. Most notably, he played Senex in a critically acclaimed performance of *A Funny Thing Happened on the Way to the Forum* at the National Theatre in Ontario, Canada. Dick got the job quite by accident, when a showgirl from his past mentioned his name to Marvin Gordon, choreographer for the show.

Gina Mallet's review of the play appeared in the January 1, 1981 edition of the *Toronto Star*. "Dick Richards is a small, drooping man with knobby knees, a pendulous lower lip, and a cracked singing voice, who quite nonchalantly steals *A Funny Thing Happened on the Way to the Forum* at the St. Lawrence Centre. Richard's role may be small, but as a veteran of the burlesque circuits, he is so completely at home in this Broadway homage to burlesque that he cannot help but set a standard. He plays Senex, an elderly Roman citizen, who wishes to improve his sex life while his large, pneumatic wife looks the other way. The ruder the jokes get, the more innocent he looks. Finally, he needs only to stand on stage managing to look sly and bewildered at the same time, to bring down the house."

Dick once said, "None of my material is new. It's been handed down over the years, and you have to doctor it up. You know, it's up to the comedian to revamp the burlesque sketches. The idea is to keep the action moving."

The small, talented comic kept the action moving, both on stage and off. For over fifty years, the fast-paced, ad-lib comedy of Dick Richards was legendary. In 1939, his career jumped from the Borscht Belt in the Catskills to the burlesque theatres in Baltimore, St. Louis, Detroit, Ohio, New York, New Jersey, Pennsylvania, and beyond. Throughout his career, Dick worked in theatres, clubs, USO shows, films, and dinner theatres. He performed on stages all across the United States, as well as in Australia and Canada.

When not on stage, Dick learned to make jewelry and he became a silversmith. He was also a painter, sculptor, an expert in antiques, as well as a gourmet chef. He enjoyed gardening, fishing, and spending time at the library. Dick loved to read. Burlesque provided a good living, and it allowed him to travel. It also introduced him to two of his three wives. He and Lorraine Lee were married for thirty-five years. She was the love of his life. Lorraine was a dancer in burlesque who also performed as a talking woman in scenes with her husband, as well as with other comics and straight men. Dick once described Lorraine as "a parade stripper, much like Ann Corio." As husband and wife, they partnered in many shows, performing in comedy bits together. Lorraine was a perfectionist when it came to harassing Dick on stage.

"He was never a gossip and he never bragged. Dick was funny—I mean really funny! He was a talented man," Lorraine once said.

One of burlesque's last top bananas, Dick died April 15, 1993, at the age of seventy-eight.

Lorraine attended several of our reunions and has always been a pleasure to be around. She provided me with the necessary material to write this chapter.

Comic Dick Richards.
PHOTO COURTESY OF: LORRAINE LEE.

Dick Richards.
PHOTO COURTESY OF: LORRAINE LEE.

**Dick and lovelies
performing comedy
bit on stage.**
PHOTO COURTESY OF:
LORRAINE LEE.

Dick Richards performing as "Senex" in the production of *A Funny Thing Happened on the Way to the Forum*, **at the Toronto State Theatre.**
PHOTO COURTESY OF: LORRAINE LEE.

G. Kukurugya and Dick Richards in a scene from *A Funny Thing Happened on the Way to the Forum*, at the Toronto State Theatre.
PHOTO COURTESY OF: LORRAINE LEE.

Lorraine Lee.
PHOTOS COURTESY OF: LORRAINE LEE.

Cutting In

(*Cast of four*)
Straight, the groom
Soubrette, the bride
Comic, the lucky one
Character, the Minister

(*The set opens in one, and then pulls to the bedroom in two.*)
Props: a bed, dressed hall tree, dresser, chair, oil can, stage money and a book or Bible.
(*The scene opens with an announcement by Straight.*)

STRAIGHT:　Ladies and gentlemen, we all know that the present generation is dance crazy and we are going to give you our conception of the "Cut In Dance" craze, which is sweeping the country. In our next little scene, for the benefit of those who do not know what the "Cut In Dance" means, I will endeavor to explain it to you. You go to a dance hall and you see a beautiful young lady that you desire to dance with. You go over and ask her for a dance and she consents. While dancing with her, and just about the time the conversation becomes interesting, some sap steps up and taps you on the back and says, "Pardon me, but do you mind if I cut in and finish this?" Naturally you have to let him finish the dance. Now ladies and gentlemen, this is our conception of the "Cut In Dance." (*Orchestra starts to play.* STRAIGHT *exits right.* COMIC *and* SOUBRETTE *enter left and start to dance. Straight re-enters, goes over to Comic, and taps him on the shoulder. Comic turns.*) I beg your pardon, do you mind if I cut in and finish this?

COMIC: (*Somewhat peeved*). Certainly not. (*Starts to exit left, walking slowly*).

STRAIGHT: You're not mad, are you?

COMIC: No, I'm not mad. (*Shows teeth and hisses*).

STRAIGHT: I was just going to tell you, if you're mad, as you pass by that icebox just help yourself to some cucumbers and ice cream. (*Comic mugs; exits left. Straight talks over his shoulder to Soubrette*). Let's Dance! (*Orchestra plays. They dance a few steps and stop*). I don't feel like dancing. Do you?

SOUBRETTE: No, I don't care to dance.

STRAIGHT: Let's do the "Why" dance. It's the latest craze. Do you know how to do it?

SOUBRETTE: I never heard of it. Show it to me.

STRAIGHT: All right I will. Put your arms around my neck. (*Soubrette does everything as directed*). Now put your other arm around my waist. Rest your head on my shoulder. Isn't this divine?

SOUBRETTE: (*Passionately*). Wonderful!

STRAIGHT: Well, why dance? Do you know I like you very much?

SOUBRETTE: And I like you too.

STRAIGHT: You wouldn't think me forward if I were to ask you for a little kiss?

SOUBRETTE: Certainly not. (*Just about to kiss when Comic enters fast from left*).

COMIC: I beg your pardon, do you mind if I cut in and finish this?

STRAIGHT: (*Peeved*). Certainly not. (*Straight starts to exit left*).

COMIC: If you're sore, as you pass that same icebox just help yourself to some strawberries and buttermilk. (*Straights then gives him a dirty look and exits left. Comic speaks to Soubrette*). Well baby, I'm back again. What do you say, you and I get hitched . . . I mean married?

SOUBRETTE: It's ok with me, baby.

COMIC: If we only had a Minister. (*Character as MINISTER steps through drop at center*). Boy, that's what I call service. Say, we want to get hitched up.

MINISTER: So you wish to be joined together in the Holy bonds of matrimony?

COMIC: Marry us and we'll get joined together later.

MINISTER: (*To Comic*) Do you take this woman in the Holy bonds of matrimony, to love, honor—

COMIC: To hell with the red tape, come on; hitch us up. (*Comic very nervous*).

MINISTER: What's the trouble son, you seem very nervous?

COMIC: Nervous hell. Anxious!

MINISTER: (*To Soubrette*) Do you take this man in the Holy bonds of matrimony, to love, honor, and cherish as long as you two shall live?

SOUBRETTE: I do.

MINISTER: I now pronounce you, man . . .

STRAIGHT: (*Comes in very fast from left*) I beg your pardon, do you mind if I cut in and finish this?

COMIC: (*Exceedingly irritated*) HELL NO!!

STRAIGHT: You're not mad, are you?

COMIC: No, I'm not mad . . . not much. I'm laughing. (*Glares and mugs*).

STRAIGHT: Well if you're mad, just get yourself some nuts and bolts.

COMIC: Some what?

STRAIGHT: Some nuts and bolts.

COMIC: Never mind the bolts. (*Mugs and exits left*).

STRAIGHT: Proceed with the ceremony.

MINISTER: Do you take this woman in the Holy bonds of matrimony, to love, honor, and cherish as long as you two shall live?

STRAIGHT: I do.

MINISTER: (*To Soubrette*) Do you take this man in the Holy bonds of matrimony to love, honor, and cherish as long as you two shall live?

SOUBRETTE: I do.

MINISTER: I now pronounce you man and wife. That will be two dollars, please.

STRAIGHT: (*Gives money*) Here you are Reverend, and here's a little tip for yourself.

MINISTER: Thank you sir; and I think it is always customary for the Minister to kiss the bride. (*Attempts to kiss Soubrette. Straight interrupts*).

STRAIGHT: I beg your pardon sir; but, do you mind if I cut in and finish this?

MINISTER: Certainly not. (*Exits right*).

STRAIGHT: Well, we are married, and you're my little wife and I'm your great big husband.

SOUBRETTE: I hope I'm not disappointed.

STRAIGHT: Well dear, let's go over to the (*name local hotel*) and spend our honeymoon there. (*Start to exit. Black out. Pull away to bedroom. Lights up*). Here we are honey, isn't this wonderful? (*Feels bed, oils springs*). Well honey, tonight's the first time for me . . .

SOUBRETTE: Oh yeah! (*Soubrette undressing*).

STRAIGHT: . . . in this room.

SOUBRETTE: Turn your back dear as I'm bashful and I don't want you to see me with my clothes off until I get into bed. (*By the time Soubrette disrobes and is in bed, Straight has coat and vest off, and then goes over and pulls down covers*).

STRAIGHT: Well dear, I'm not going to bother undressing. I'm afraid of fire. (*Just about to get into bed when Comic enters through center drape*).

COMIC: Pardon me, do you mind if I cut in and finish this?

(Black out.)

Snap Your Fingers

(*Time: 7 or 8 minutes*)
Cast of five:
Straight, gets a telegram
Soubrette, his sweetheart
Character Woman, a sweet old lady
Character Man, a doubtful old man
Comic, their son

(*Props: table, cover, two chairs, settee, dresser, hall tree, telegram, suitcase, handbag, magazine, pipe and tobacco*).
(*Scene One: In the street. SOUBRETTE enters from left. STRAIGHT enters from right. They meet center and greet each other. Straight takes telegram from pocket*).

STRAIGHT:	I just received a letter from my brother Jake who has been away for the past year in one of those hypnotic schools where he has been studying hypnotism. Listen to what he says . . . (*reads*) . . . will be home sometime this evening, so tell the folks.
SOUBRETTE:	Oh isn't that wonderful, your brother is a hypnotist. I wonder if he can really hypnotize people?
STRAIGHT:	I don't know, but come let's hurry home. I want to inform the folks that he will arrive this evening. (*Both exit left*).

(Scene Two: Interior of a sitting room. Pull away to set in two. OLD MAN seated at table reading a book and smoking a pipe. WOMAN standing at table. HUSBAND seated directly behind her reading. Smells pipe, looks at shoe, looks at floor, woman's pratt, mugs).

OLD MAN: Hey Ma . . .

OLD WOMAN: Yes?

OLD MAN: Just looking at the scenery from the rear kind of makes me feel young again. Ain't felt like this in years. Raring to go and can't go for raring.

OLD WOMAN: Why you old goat, you've been dead from the waist down for the past twenty years.

OLD MAN: Has it been that long, ma?

OLD WOMAN: You know damn well it has.

OLD MAN: Don't seem that long. Time sure does fly.

STRAIGHT: *(Straight and Soubrette enter from left)* Hello Ma. Hello Pa. I just received a telegram, and guess who it's from?

OLD MAN: Don't know unless it's the sheriff.

STRAIGHT: Nope, it's from Jake, and he'll be home sometime this evening.

OLD WOMAN: Oh, from Jake. My boy will be home this evening!

OLD MAN: Coming home today.

STRAIGHT: Yep.

OLD MAN:	Ma, I better go out right now and lock up the sheep. (*Pause*) Damn, Jake. Two years in college. What the hell is he going to be?
STRAIGHT:	He's studying hypnotism.
OLD MAN:	Heard of rheumatism. Anything like that?
STRAIGHT:	No, it's in the mind . . . a mental case.
OLD MAN:	That's Jake all right. He's a mental case if there ever was one.
STRAIGHT:	Yes mother, he should be a full fledge hypnotist by this time. Gee, I'll be glad to see him.
OLD WOMAN:	So will I!
OLD MAN:	I'll be glad to see him all right, but I'll bet he's a fake.
OLD WOMAN:	My boy is not a fake. I'll bet he can hypnotize anybody! (*Noise off right*).
STRAIGHT:	I'll bet that's Jake coming now. (COMIC *enters very fast with suitcase in hand. Throws it to one side. Rushes over to Old Woman and embraces her*).
COMIC:	Hello Ma!
OLD WOMAN:	Hello Son! (*Comic greets Straight, his brother, then Mother again. Buries head in Mother's breast*).
OLD MAN:	What in the hell are you doing? Ain't you weaned yet? Damn good thing you ain't a midget!

COMIC:	(*Goes from Old Woman to Old Man, who by this time is standing*). Hello Pa!
OLD MAN:	Hello Son. Glad to see you!
COMIC:	Glad to see you too, but sit down you old fossil before you fall down. (*Crosses to Straight at right*). Hello Bill!
STRAIGHT:	Hello Jake! Good to see you again. Guess by this time you are a full-fledged hypnotist?
COMIC:	Oh yes, I'm there now. I can hypnotize anybody.
STRAIGHT:	Can you hypnotize me?
COMIC:	Why certainly.
STRAIGHT:	I'll bet you can't do it.
COMIC:	Oh, I can all right. I don't want to put you to sleep, but I'll tell you what I will do. I'll put any part of your body to sleep. Hold out your arm. (*Straight does so*). Now watch this. (*Comic makes a few passes, says a few words, jerking business. While hypnotizing, Straight holds arm rigid*). Here you are. Now try and move your arm. (*Straight tries, but holds arm rigid*).
STRAIGHT:	I can't. It's stiff!
COMIC:	I told you. Now the only way to limber it up is for me to snap my fingers. Watch. (*Comic snaps fingers. Straight lets arm fall to side, then shakes it*).
STRAIGHT:	Say, that's all right.

OLD WOMAN: Son, can you do that to me?

COMIC: Certainly. Hold out your leg. (*Old Woman holds out leg. Comic makes passes. Same business*). Now try and move your leg. (*Old Woman tries, but can't*).

OLD WOMAN: I can't.

COMIC: Wait till I snap my fingers. (*Snaps; Old Woman lets leg fall*).

OLD MAN: He's still a damn fake. You two are in cahoots with him. I send him to college for two years to learn how to do that? (*Jerk*) He done that back of the barn, before he went to college.

SOUBRETTE: Can you do that to me?

COMIC: (*Sees Soubrette for the first time*) Hello Helene. (*To Straight*) See you still got the same old girl.

STRAIGHT: Yep.

COMIC: Think I'll put her to sleep, and then come around the house some evening.

STRAIGHT: No, No!!

SOUBRETTE: Come on, hypnotize me!

COMIC: All right, I'll hypnotize your neck. (*Makes pass; same business. Soubrette holds neck stiff*). There you are. Move your head.

SOUBRETTE: I can't.

COMIC: All right here you are. (*Snaps fingers; Soubrette moves neck*). Well dad, what do you think of it?

OLD MAN: Well you may be able to do it to them, but I'll bet you can't do it to me. I'm from Missouri!

COMIC: Why dad, I can make any part of your body stiff.

OLD MAN: (*Mugs this. Gets up*) Let me get this right. (*Whispers in son's ear*).

COMIC: Why certainly, stand still. (*Passes words. Old Man stands for a minute; mugs*).

OLD MAN: Damned if you ain't right!

COMIC: I told you I was! Well I may as well . . . (*Goes to snap fingers. Old Man sees him.*)

OLD MAN: (*Yelling*) Wait a minute! Hot damn! You wait a minute!

COMIC: What's the trouble pop?

OLD MAN: Son, if you love your mother, don't snap them fingers!!

(Black out).

You'll Have to Ask the Old Lady

(*Cast of three and chorus: as many girls as possible to cross stage, all wearing aprons and sun bonnets*).

Character, the farmer
Straight, the traveling man
Character Woman, the old woman

(*Set: farm drop in two. Set: house with practical door on right*).
(*Props: bench, milk bucket, briefcase, pocket knife, and whitlin' stick.*)
(*At opening,* FARMER *is seated on bench center, whitlin'.* STRAIGHT *enters left and addresses farmer*).

STRAIGHT: I beg your pardon sir, but I'm a traveling salesman, and I'm in a little trouble. My automobile broke down just about a mile down the road, and I'll be unable to make the next town, which is about fifteen miles away. Could you possibly put me up for the night?

FARMER: I don't know. You'll have to ask the old lady. (WIFE *enters from house*).

STRAIGHT: I beg your pardon ma'am, but could you put me up here for the night?

WIFE: (*Looks Straight over*) I reckon we can.

STRAIGHT: Thank you ma'am. (*Wife exits into house. Straight looks place over, then turns to Farmer*). Mighty big farm you have here. How many acres have you?

FARMER: I don't know. You'll have to ask the old woman.

WIFE: 175.

STRAIGHT: All in crops?

WIFE: No, we have 25 acres of wheat, 50 acres of corn . . . (*Glares at Farmer*) . . . and one stinkweed! (*She exits back of house. Farmer looks at wife, then at Straight and mugs*).

STRAIGHT: One stinkweed and she looked right at you. You're in good.

FARMER: Sure am.

STRAIGHT: (*Points left*) On my way up here I saw quite a few cattle down in the meadow. How many head do you have?

FARMER: I don't know. You'll have to ask the old woman. (*Wife comes from behind the house*).

STRAIGHT: I beg your pardon ma'am, how many head of cattle have you?

WIFE: Well, we have 200 head of beef, about 75 head of sheep, 25 . . . (*Looks at Farmer again*) . . . and one sow! (*Exits into house*).

STRAIGHT: One sow! Again she looked right at you.

FARMER: Yep, she means me.

STRAIGHT: (*Looks around again*) How many fruit trees have you?

FARMER: I don't know. You'll have to ask the old lady. (*Wife enters from house*).

STRAIGHT: I beg your pardon, how many fruit trees have you?

WIFE: 15 acres of pears, 25 acres of peaches, 10 acres of russet apples . . . (*Glares at Farmer*) . . . and one crab! (*Exits behind house*).

FARMER: (*mugs*) One crab!! I'm lucky.

STRAIGHT: Any pets around the house?

FARMER: Pets?

STRAIGHT: Yes, you know, dogs, cats . . . .

FARMER: I don't know. You'll have to ask the old lady. (*Wife enters from behind house*).

STRAIGHT: Have you any pets around ma'am?

WIFE: We have three dogs, two cats . . . (*Looks at Farmer*) . . . and one old skunk!

FARMER: Hell, I ain't an old skunk!

(*As many GIRLS as possible cross the stage left to right. As they pass, each says "Hello dad" or "Hello pop." They exit into the house. Straight looks amazed*).

STRAIGHT: Mighty fine looking bunch of girls. Are you the father of all them girls?

FARMER: I don't know. You'll have to ask the old lady!
(Black out).

A Sampling of Burlesque Theatres

Preserving as much information as possible about historical old theatres is important. If we do not do it, the information may be lost forever. Perhaps this chapter will wet your whistle and intrigue you enough to research those theatres that still stand. So many glorious old structures have already been dismantled and torn down to create beautiful, asphalt parking lots. Is the monetary difference is so great that the few remaining theatres can't be preserved for the benefit of our children and grandchildren? My goal is to make people more aware. I am sure that many additional pieces of the theatre puzzle will be put together in time, something the Theatre Historical Society of America has been striving to do for many years.

I discovered that locating theatre information is sometimes confusing and difficult. Names often changed, and over the years, many theatres used several different names. What follows is a partial listing of just some of those theatres in which old-time performers recall having played burlesque shows. These have been documented with articles in newspapers, books, and publications, including old Billboard magazines. Some owners of existing theatres ignore their burlesque history, but the Folly Theater in Kansas City, Missouri, is proud of their burlesque history, as Kate Egan discovered when she worked for and researched the facility. I only wish more owners and managers would research their theatre's history and acknowledge their past.

MOULIN ROUGE THEATRE
OAKLAND, CALIFORNIA

In 1909, the Gem Theatre was built at 485 8th Street. The theatre had 376 seats. In 1933, it was renamed the Moulin Rouge. It featured a marquee with revolving neon and a metal windmill that remained in place until the theatre was demolished. Mona Vaughn remembered performing from the 1930s through the 1950s in burlesque shows at this theatre. Like many old theatres, it began showing adult films in the 1960s, and closed sometime in the early 1970s.

BURBANK THEATRE
LOS ANGELES, CALIFORNIA

In 1893, the Burbank Theatre was built at 548 South Main by Dr. David Burbank. The theatre had 1,027 seats. In 1899, producer Oliver Morosco leased the theatre, but in 1913, he opened his own Morosco Theatre, later to be called the Globe Theatre. In the 1930s, the Burbank was turned into a newsreel house. By the 1950s, it was known for its burlesque shows called the *Burbank Follies*. Prior to being demolished in 1973, it showcased adult films.

Burlesque comic Billy Reed at Burbank Theatre War Bond Rally on December 15, 1941.
PHOTO COURTESY OF: MIMI REED.

Group photo from Burbank Theatre War Bond Rally held on December 15, 1941. From left to right: Herbie Barris, Billy Reed, Dorothy Darling, John Crawford, Vicki "Babe" Davis, Mimi Reed, Louise Miller, Johnny Maloney, and Jack Murray.
PHOTO COURTESY OF: MIMI REED.

Burbank Theatre Los Angeles, California.
PHOTO COURTESY OF: BURLESQUE HISTORICAL SOCIETY.

FOLLIES THEATRE
LOS ANGELES, CALIFORNIA

In 1901, the Follies Theatre was built (some reports state 1904) at 327 North Main Street by David Belasco. It had 900 seats, and was originally named after Belasco. During those years, Main Street was the heart of the theatre district and the city was alive with vaudeville. Visiting thespians at the theatre included Laurette Taylor, Charles Ruggles, Lewis Stone, Marjorie Rambeau, Hobart Bosworth, and W. C. Fields. By 1925, the city began to expand west and the theatre district moved to Broadway, where theatres ran vaudeville shows, as well as movies. The Belasco marquee was removed and used at a theatre on Hill Street. The Main Street Theatre became a house of burlesque and was renamed the Follies.

In 1937, the theatre was used in the Mae West film, *Every Day's a Holiday*, but as years progressed, people lined up to see some of the biggest and best burlesque shows on the West coast. The Follies offered elaborate revues with a large chorus line, fancy costumes, full orchestra, specialty numbers, comedic interludes, and of course, ecdysiasts. Joe Yule Sr., father of Mickey Rooney, was the favorite top banana, and Betty Rowland, the "Ball of Fire," frequently served as a much-appreciated feature attraction. It was a colorful place, and the theatre's history included numerous reports of raids, disputes, trials, scandals, publicity gimmicks, and even genuine tragedy.

Backstage at the Follies, among the jumbled clutter of torn and faded scenery, stray lighting equipment, discarded costumes, props, and broken bulletin boards, a ghost named Alice was rumored to reside. Burlesque performers working at the theatre often told tales of strange noises and activities, and for years, one story continued regarding a dancer often seen being pulled from the chorus line into the wings by invisible hands. Some believed it was Alice, a former chorus line dancer, who many alleged was murdered by her jealous boyfriend.

World War Two and the Korean Conflict brought in servicemen by the truckloads and business was brisk. Defense bonds were even sold in the theatre. However, by the late 1960s, burlesque shows with production numbers and comedy skits were history. The small audiences, who then occupied the once-luxurious seats, watched a vast assortment of dancers quickly strip off their clothes, while a three-piece band provided accompaniment. The Follies Theatre was continually raided, closed, and reopened before management finally replaced the strippers and band in the early 1970s with adult movies. In 1974, the musty old theatre was demolished and replaced by a parking lot.

Follies Theatre, Los Angeles, California.
PHOTO COURTESY OF: BURLESQUE HISTORICAL SOCIETY.

CAPITOL THEATRE
SAN FRANCISCO, CALIFORNIA

In 1911, the Cort Theatre first opened at 64 Ellis Street. It seated 3,000, and it featured live stage productions. In 1918, it was renamed the Curran. In 1921, it became known as the Century. In 1922, it was renamed the Morosco. In 1923, it finally became known as the Capitol.

In the 1930s, it became a popular burlesque house and home to the *Capitol Follies.* In June 1941, it closed and was torn down.

Originally built as the Cort Theatre in 1911, it was renamed the Capitol in 1923.
PHOTO COURTESY OF: BURLESQUE HISTORICAL SOCIETY.

DOWNTOWN THEATRE
SAN FRANCISCO, CALIFORNIA

In 1917, the Casino Theatre opened at 198 Ellis Street, presenting vaudeville shows and films. It held 1,934 seats. The theatre prospered until talking pictures were introduced, and then it struggled through the depression by showing B movies.

In 1942, it reopened as the Downtown Theatre, showing double features that changed daily. In 1950, the theatre became a house of burlesque, and it survived two more years before finally closing for good in September 1952.

In 1953, the Downtown Theatre was demolished.

Liberty Theatre
San Francisco, California

In 1909, the California Theatre originally opened in San Francisco's North Beach District. It seated 800. In 1910, it was renamed the Liberty Theatre. Around 1920, it became know as the Allies Theatre. In the mid-1920s, it was renamed the Crescent Theatre.

In 1926, its name was changed back to the Liberty Theatre. In 1941, when the Capitol Theatre closed, the *Capitol Follies* burlesque shows moved to the Liberty Theatre. Throughout the 1940s, the theatre prospered due to large numbers of military personnel based in the area during World War Two, but its burlesque days ended after the war. In March 1949, it was re-christened the World Theatre and began showing foreign films. In April 1953 it was closed and torn down; but the name of the Verdi Theatre across the street changed to the World Theatre, and management continued presenting foreign films.

President Follies Theatre
San Francisco, California

In 1905, construction began on the Colonial Theatre at 60 McAllister Street. It had 990 seats. Construction was delayed by the San Francisco earthquake and fire, and the Colonial Theatre did not formally open until October 6, 1906. In 1909, it was renamed the Savoy Theatre. It has been reported that in 1912, Lon Chaney Sr., made his stage debut at the theatre, which went through many name changes. In 1913, it was called the Oriental Theatre, and in 1916, it was renamed the Savoy Theatre. In 1922, it was called the Plaza Theatre, and finally in May 1925, it was re-christened the President Theatre, which it remained until the theatre closed.

During the 1920s, the President Theatre continued offering live stage productions. However, between the onslaughts of theatres converting from silent to talking pictures, the 1929 stock market crash, and the Great Depression, the theatre's future looked bleak. In 1941, Eddie Skolak turned the theatre into the President Follies, a popular house of burlesque, which served San Francisco area audiences throughout World War Two, the 1950s, and into the 1960s. After Skolak's death, his widow sold the theatre in September 1963 and permanently closed the doors. Soon afterward, it was torn down.

ADAMS THEATRE
CHICAGO, ILLINOIS

In 1921, the Adams Theatre opened at 20 East Adams Street. It was one of the smaller theatres in the Chicago Loop, and it had seating for only 600 people. Initially, it was operated by Vista Amusement Enterprises, and then in 1930, it switched to exhibiting newsreel and short features. For a short time, the *Minsky Follies*, produced by Harold Minsky, showcased their productions at the Adams Theatre, but the theatre closed long ago, and it has since been demolished.

RIALTO THEATRE
CHICAGO, ILLINOIS

In 1917, the Rialto Theatre opened at 336 South State Street. It was designed in the Renaissance Revival style by the architectural duo of Marshall and Fox, who also designed the Blackstone Theatre, Blackstone Hotel, and later, the Drake Hotel. It held 1,548 seats. It was built for the Jones, Linick, and Schaefer Circuit, which also included the Orpheum Theatre, the Randolph Theatre, and the Plaza Theatre.

The Rialto Theatre served as a venue for vaudeville and motion pictures, but by the 1930s, the theatre became famous as a house of burlesque. By the late 1960s, the name was changed to the Downtown Theatre and it showed adult films. In the late 1970s, it was torn down.

STAR AND GARTER THEATRE
CHICAGO, ILLINOIS

In 1908, the Star and Garter Theatre opened at 815 West Madison Street. It operated as a burlesque theatre, but it also showcased vaudeville performances. It had seating for 1,500. In later years, it became a movie theatre. In 1973, the Star and Garter Theatre was demolished and replaced with a parking lot.

STATE-CONGRESS THEATRE
CHICAGO, ILLINOIS

Around 1910, the U. S. Music Hall opened at 546 South State Street near Congress Parkway in Chicago's South Loop. It originally served as a vaudeville theatre and concert hall, but was also used to screen movies. When it was renamed the State-Congress Theatre, it also changed its venue to burlesque, which continued until the theatre closed sometime around 1950. It has been reported that the first striptease was performed on the State-Congress stage in 1928 by Hinda Wassau.

Hinda Wassau, relaxing backstage in her dressing room.
PHOTO COURTESY OF: LEE STUART.

GAIETY THEATRE
BOSTON, MASSACHUSETTS

In 1908, the New Lyceum Theatre was designed by leading theatre architect Clarence Blackall and built at 659-665 Washington Street. It showcased vaudeville and vaudeville style, clean burlesque shows. It had two balconies and seating for 1,700 people.

Opening night took place on November 23, 1908, and all 1,700 seats were filled. Patrons paid 10¢ for a seat in the gallery and $1 for a box seat. Matinee and evening performances were held at 2:15 pm and 8 pm. The name was changed to the Gaiety Theatre, and it was last theatre built specifically for burlesque in Boston. The theatre had a simple design, no ornate street marquee or façade, and its acoustic virtues were outstanding.

In the 1920s, the theatre not only was a venue for burlesque, but along with the Casino Theatre, it also presented the African-American *Harlem Renaissance Shows.* The Gaiety was the only theatre in New England where African-American vaudevillians and performers could entertain. Josephine Baker, Moms Mabley, a very young Sammy Davis Jr., Dewey "Pigmeat" Markham, Buck & Bubbles, a team performing from 1912 to 1953, Florence Mills, and Julia Moody all performed at the Gaiety Theatre for racially mixed audiences. At that time, most audiences remained segregated. By 1930, these shows gave way to the pressure of the Great Depression, but during that era of racial intolerance, theatres like the Gaiety offered African-American talent of all types a place to showcase their work, create professional reputations, and earn a respectable living.

The Gaiety was closed for more than 20 years by 2005. It was a second-rate movie house showing Kung Fu movies and adult films before that. No live performances had been held in the theatre since before World War Two.

On January 5, 2005, a local Bostonian sent me the following e-mail: "The more I have been reading up on the Gaiety Theatre, in my opinion it is a complete disgrace how the owners of the building have apparently greased the palms of our local politicians and the Boston Redevelopment Authority to be able to tear it down. What a shame! There are several groups still fighting the demolition, which is why it is still standing."

Though gutted, the theatre was reported to be in excellent structural condition. However, in early 2005, it was scheduled to be demolished in order to make way for a thirty-story luxury apartment complex. An organization known as the Friends of the Gaiety Theatre continued their fight to save the building, but time ran out and it was destroyed.

As historians, we must continue to work together to help remaining theatres in other communities survive. Our cultural resources must be preserved, not destroyed. Friends of the Gaiety Theatre can be reached at www.gaietyboston.com. Photos of the demolition can be found at their web site, as well. It is sad to see such an end come to a wonderful old historical theatre.

NATIONAL THEATRE
DETROIT, MICHIGAN

In 1911, the National Theatre opened at 118 Monroe Street as a vaudeville house. It was designed by architect Albert Kahn in an Art Nouveau style with Egyptian elements. The polychrome, terra cotta façade was stunning, and the exterior featured a large window that resembled a triumphant arch and showcased two minarets on either side, which were topped by gilded domes. Nature-based décor, including stylized scarab beetles and floral designs also adorned the façade. The interior originally had seating for 2,200, and featured a large stage with a simple yet elegant décor.

It opened as a vaudeville theatre, but within only a few short years, it switched to movies. By the 1940s, it became a house of burlesque. In the 1960s, it was renamed the Palace Theatre and began showing adult films. In 1975, the theatre closed.

GAYETY THEATRE
MINNEAPOLIS, MINNESOTA

In 1909, Herman Faehr opened the Gayety Theatre at 103 North Washington Avenue. It was designed in Neo-Classical style, and seated just over 1,200 people. The façade was made of luminous white terra cotta, and it featured a pediment that was held up by a quartet of Corinthian pillars. Inside, the proscenium arch rose seventy feet above the stage.

The Gayety Theatre was originally a legitimate theatre, but by the mid teens, the theatre had switched to vaudeville and burlesque shows. During the 1920s, Al Jolson, Fanny Brice, and Sophie Tucker all played the Gayety Theatre. In 1928, the city of Minneapolis closed the theatre after deciding that shows had become too racy. It was only after management promised to showcase musical comedy acts onstage rather than burlesque that the theatre was allowed to reopen the following year.

In 1941, after decades of live entertainment, the Gayety Theatre finally turned to showing movies. Late in 1941, the theatre was renamed the Floyd B. Olson Theatre after a popular Minnesota governor of the 1920s and 1030s, who died in 1936. However, when Olson's widow learned that her husband's name brightly lit up the marquee of a former house of burlesque, she sued the theatre. Management immediately changed the name back to the Gayety Theatre, and Mrs. Olson dropped her suit.

In the mid 1940s, the theatre closed again. Plans were discussed to convert the Gayety Theatre into a nightclub, but the plans fell through. Then in 1970, after sitting vacant for decades, it was announced that the theatre would be restored, but once again, nothing came of the plans. Around 1980, the theatre was torn down.

EMPRESS THEATRE
KANSAS CITY, MISSOURI

In May 1910, the Empress Theatre opened at 1120-24 McGee Street. It was designed by Kansas City architect Carl Bolter and built by the Sullivan and Considine Vaudeville Circuit. It had seating for 1,902 people, and was considered one of the most modern vaudeville houses in America. The fireproofed structure of concrete, steel, marble, and tile cost $180,000 to build and opened with three vaudeville and motion picture shows, daily. Controversy over the film, *Ecstasy*, threatened to close the theatre, but it played on despite the critics.

With the decline of vaudeville, the theatre became a house of burlesque. In late 1936, it closed after a proposed forty-week burlesque season lasted only twelve weeks. The building was remodeled and converted into several individual stores. In 1956, the entire structure was torn down to build a parking garage.

Folly Theater
Kansas City, Missouri

On September 23, 1900, the Standard Theatre and adjoining Edward Hotel were designed by Louis S. Curtiss. Edward Butler, a prominent businessman from St. Louis, commissioned the theatre in hopes of creating a national chain. The theatre opened at 300 West 12th Street at the center of the city's theatre district, which included fourteen legitimate theatres. It held seating for 600 people. The theatre was designed as a true spectacle. A giant ball of lights affixed to a pole on the roof descended and remained brightly lit while the theatre was in use. The light-colored pressed-brick façade was adorned with a variety of galvanized metal ornamentation, and a triple-arch window, inspired by Andrea Palladio, a 16th-century Italian sculpture and architect, was also a prominent feature. Curtiss used soft pastels, intricate plasterwork, and magnificent chandeliers to finish his interior design. The Edward Hotel became a meeting place for actors, producers, newspapermen, and other persons associated with the theatre industry.

The first show to play the theatre was *The Jolly Grass Widow*, a polite burlesque starring Madame Diks. The theatre became known for burlesque, vaudeville, and comedy performances. In January 1901, when the Coates Opera House caught on fire, performances scheduled for that theatre moved to the Standard Theatre. In 1902, the Standard Theatre was renamed the Century Theatre.

Famous performers, such as Maude Adams, Richard Mansfield, Sarah Bernhardt, Al Jolson, Fanny Brice, Eddie Foy, and the Marx Brothers, all entertained audiences during the first decade of the theatre's existence.

In May 1920, after a fire destroyed much of the theatre's upper balcony, the Shubert's bought the building and completed a $25,000 renovation. It reopened as Shubert's Missouri Theatre, and presented classical drama, including works by Shakespeare and Eugene O'Neill. For the next decade, the theatre struggled to stay alive. In 1932, with huge bills piling up, dwindling attendance, and the onslaught of the Great Depression, the owners closed its doors.

In 1941, Barney Allis bought the theatre and reopened it as the Folly. Efforts were made to reestablish vaudeville shows, but the Folly soon became known as a house of burlesque. Dancers, comics, straight men, and a few variety acts, which normally toured the circuit, began performing their routine five shows a day at the theatre. Famous exotic dancers, including Gypsy Rose Lee and Sally Rand, who mastered the art of suggestion rather than employing total, blatant nudity in their act, all took turns performing at the theatre, which then was known as the Folly Burlesk.

A group of censors upholding local laws monitored the goings-on in burlesque theatres and quickly began regulating the shows at the Folly Burlesk. A bulletin board noted: "Women must wear net pants and brassieres. Brassieres must have cover for nipples. No bumps or grinds direct to the audience. No hanging on curtains. Do not touch body. No extreme flash. Wear panels. No suggestive lyrics in any vocal numbers! This is local law and they are very strict."

Society changed, and so changed the restrictions. The Edward Hotel was razed in 1965, and shows at the Folly Burlesk became increasingly vulgar. By the late 1960s, strippers could no longer compete with the adult film industry, and burlesque ceased to be profitable.

On the morning of December 28, 1969, a headline on the *Kansas City Star* read, "Old Grind Gets Bumped at Folly Theater Here." The article reported, "The plan was to replace the show girls with showings of adult art films."

In 1970, the Folly Burlesk was in a financial free-fall. The theatre was not being maintained, yet despite plunging audiences, adult films continued to be shown until January 23, 1974, when the theatre "died a quiet death," according to a January 24, 1974 article in the *Kansas City Star.*

The Folly Burlesk was sold to a New York property management company to be torn down to make room for a new parking lot. However, concerned citizens led by Joan Dillon created the Performing Arts Foundation, whose goal was to preserve the Folly Theater—the last, legitimate, turn-of-the-century theatre in Kansas City. The Foundation acquired the property for $500,000, and before the end of 1974, the building was listed on the National Register of Historic Places.

In November 1981, the restored Folly Theater reopened, and the first performance was a musical revue by musician, Carole King.

The Folly continues to host a variety of performing artists, live shows, and other fine arts activities. For more information or to support the Folly Theater, visit www.follytheater.com.

Between 1941 and 1974 the theatre was simply called Folly Burlesk. In 1981 the historical building was renamed the Folly Theater.
PHOTO COURTESY OF: FOLLY THEATER ARCHIVES, KANSAS CITY, MISSOURI. (KATE EGAN)

Folly Burlesk, 1965.
PHOTO COURTESY OF:
LEE STUART.

GARRICK THEATRE
ST. LOUIS, MISSOURI

In 1904, the Garrick Theatre was designed by architect W. Albert Swasey and constructed at a cost of $350,000 at 515 Chestnut Street in the heart of downtown St. Louis. It was named after famed actor David Garrick. Its distinctive turn-of-the-century façade featured stone-front arched doorways and a modest marquee that simply read "Garrick Theatre" on each side. The theatre was small but attractive, and had seating for nearly 800. It served as a legitimate playhouse until World War One.

The Shubert Brothers' involvement made the Garrick Theatre successful. They brought in such notable performers as Al Jolson and Fanny Brice. After World War One, the Garrick Theatre could no longer compete with vaudeville and movies. The theatre turned to burlesque, which proved to be a profitable venture into the 1940s.

After World War Two, the Garrick Theatre changed to showing adult films. By then, the building was in a serious state of disrepair. The interior was rundown and had cracked plaster throughout the auditorium. The seats were in dire need of reupholstering and the floor badly needed repairs. In October 1954, the Garrick Theatre was demolished.

GAYETY THEATRE
KANSAS CITY, MISSOURI

In 1909, the Gayety Theatre was designed by architect Carl Bolter and erected on the site of the former residence of meat packing magnate A. W. Armour on the southeast corner of 12th and Wyandotte. It was built of reinforced concrete and ornamental stone, and it held seats for 1,600 people. 570 seats were on the orchestra floor, 100 seats were in boxes, 400 seats were in the balcony, and 500 seats were in the gallery. The building also housed several stores at ground floor and seventeen offices on the second floor.

The Gayety Theatre owners were former operators of the Majestic Theatre, a well-known local house of burlesque. They booked burlesque shows as the main feature in their new theatre. In 1927, a dancer's performance was declared "immoral and indecent" and led to an injunction against the theatre owners. The Gayety Theatre operated as a theatre until 1935. In the 1940s, a popular nightclub called the College Inn was housed in the Gayety Building. In 1950, the structure was torn down to make way for an expansion of the Muehlebach Hotel.

EMPIRE THEATRE
NEWARK, NEW JERSEY

In 1912, the Empire Theatre opened at 265 Washington Street. It had seating for nearly 1,000 people. It was beautifully built, and it included a long balcony that brought the upstairs patrons closer to the stage by seating them directly over the customers sitting in the higher priced, main floor orchestra seats. The theatre originally opened as a variety show house, but in the late 1920s when vaudeville began losing its audiences to motion pictures, burlesque shows were added to the bill. Striptease was just what the Empire Theatre needed to lure men away from the movies.

According to an old Empire Theatre playbill, admission prices were as low as 30¢. Shows that played the theatre were units of a touring circuit that performed at the Empire Theatre for one week and then moved on to the next city. Each unit included everything necessary for that particular show: comics, exotic dancers, straight men, house singers, chorus lines, scenery, and variety acts. All the Empire Theatre provided was the building.

All the famous strippers from the 1930s and 1940s played the Empire Theatre, including Margie Hart, Lili St. Cyr, Rosita Royce, and Georgia Sothern. In the late 1930s, the theatre enjoyed an unexpected surge of business after Mayor Fiorella LaGuardia closed the theatres in New York City, which drove burlesque fans across the Hudson River to the Empire Theatre in Newark and the Hudson Theatre in Union City.

By the 1950s, television, supper clubs, and motion pictures reduced attendance at all burlesque theatres. Simultaneously, anti-burlesque amendments were added to Newark's theatre ordinances making it nearly impossible to continue. Then, with the arrest of twenty-one burlesque performers and a license revocation threatened by the city, the Empire Theatre closed its doors on February 14, 1957. In July 1958, the Empire Theatre was torn down to create a parking lot for downtown Newark shoppers.

Empire Theatre Newark, New Jersey.
PHOTO COURTESY OF: BURLESQUE HISTORICAL SOCIETY.

Partial photo of the Empire Theatre marquee in Newark, New Jersey.
PHOTO COURTESY OF: MARA GAYE & THE SIEGFRIED FAMILY.

Poster for Empire Theatre burlesque show starring Peaches and Mara Gaye.
PHOTO COURTESY OF: MARA GAYE & THE SIEGFRIED FAMILY.

Hudson Theatre
Union City, New Jersey

In the 1930s, as vaudeville began its decline, B. F. Keith's Hudson Theatre on 38th Street in Union City, New Jersey changed hands and became the Hudson Burlesque Theatre. Popular with performers and patrons alike, stars such as Phil Silvers, Bert Lahr, Ann Corio, and Abbott & Costello all performed at the Hudson Theatre.

In October 1957, three strippers were arrested for violating a newly imposed "no strip" ordinance, and a week later, the Hudson Burlesque Theatre closed for good.

"Burlesque was family entertainment, where fellows brought their gals to see stars and to still have a little naughty fun on a Saturday night," said Joan Torino, a former Hudson Theatre dancer and member of The Golden Days of Burlesque Historical Society. The theatre was torn down to make room for, what else, a parking lot.

Hudson Theatre marquee, Union City, New Jersey.
Photo courtesy of: Mara Gaye & the Siegfried family.

FROM LEFT TO RIGHT:
Athena, deceased; Maria Bradley, Joan Torino, deceased; Hope Diamond, and Ellye O'Connell—all Hudson Theatre girls.
PHOTO COURTESY OF: MARIA BRADLEY.

PICTURED RIGHT FROM LEFT TO RIGHT:
Hudson Theatre owner Sam Cohen, and Paul DeSavino Sr., head stagehand at the Hudson for over 30 years.
PHOTO COURTESY OF: PAUL DESAVINO JR.

FROM LEFT TO RIGHT:
Eppie O'Kean, manager of the Hudson Burlesque Theatre, and his brother Dave Kane, a stagehand at the theatre.
PHOTO COURTESY OF: PAUL DESAVINO JR.

FIFTH AVENUE THEATRE
NEW YORK, NEW YORK

In 1865, the Fifth Avenue Opera House opened on 24th Street. In 1873, that structure burned down. The theatre was rebuilt in the old Apollo Hall at 27-31 West 28th Street. In 1891, that theatre also burned down. It was promptly rebuilt on the same site. The theatre held 1530 seats. Architect Francis Hatch Kimball designed the Fifth Avenue Theatre in a highly ornate style with terra-cotta decoration that almost covered the entire 28th Street entrance, which became the side entrance. The entrance on Broadway became the main entryway, but it was not as lavishly decorated.

The 28th Street lobby was decorated with various shades of marble walls, gilded columns, elaborate plasterwork, and intricate stained glass windows. The halls were lined with marble columns and mirrors that added a feeling of depth to the narrow space. Persian carpets, imported draperies, and decorative artwork added to the luxurious surroundings.

Inside the auditorium, the décor was a mixture of Neo-Classical and Neo-Baroque Renaissance styles. It was extensively decorated with gilt plasterwork and painted in shades of ivory with gold trim. Unlike other theatres, the new Fifth Avenue Theatre had rows of seats rather than benches on the orchestra floor and in the balconies, which by the end of the 19th Century, were considered old-fashioned.

The theatre was built with the latest innovations, including electric lighting, fireproof materials, and minimal balcony support columns that maintained a better view of the stage. The impressive new theatre was far from Longacre Square (the name later changed to Times Square), which was then the heart of the theatre district. By 1900, the Fifth Avenue Theatre had staged its last legitimate show.

The theatre was soon leased by F. F. Proctor for his vaudeville circuit, and by 1915, it was showing motion pictures, in addition to showcasing vaudeville acts. After 1929, burlesque shows became the main venue. In 1939, the theatre was demolished to make way for an office building.

New Victory Theatre
New York, New York

In 1900, the Theatre Republic was built by J. B. McElfatrick and Sons at 229 West 42nd Street. It held nearly 500 seats, and it presented legitimate theatre productions. In 1902, David Belasco leased the theatre and renamed it the Belasco. By 1914, the theatre had been renamed the Republic Theatre, and continued its run as a legitimate theatre.

In 1932, it became a house of burlesque, but it was not Broadway's first burlesque theatre. The Columbia Theatre had opened in 1910 at Broadway and 47th Street, and it presented burlesque shows well into the 1920s.

The Republic Theatre became home to *Minsky's Follies* until Mayor Fiorello LaGuardia shut the theatre down during his very public crackdown on vice in New York City during the late 1930s and into the early 1940s. In the early 1940s, the theatre reopened and was renamed the Victory Theatre due to the surge of patriotism felt across the nation during World War Two, and it began showing second-run movies.

In the 1970s, the Victory Theatre fell on tough times and became the first theatre on Broadway to show X-rated films, which continued into the late 1980s. In 1990, in an effort to revitalize 42nd Street, the Victory Theatre came under public ownership. In August 1994, the theatre was leased to a non-profit organization. Renovations began and were completed in December 1995 at a cost of over $11 million. The restored theatre re-opened, providing family orientated entertainment and representing what communities could do when they worked together to preserve local history. For over 100 years, the New Victory Theatre has been a feature on the ever-changing backdrop of New York City's celebrated 42nd Street.

Roxy Theatre
Cleveland, Ohio

In 1906, the property at 1882 East 9th Street was leased by Truman Swetland from Levi Meachum for a total of ninety-nine years. In 1907, the Family Theatre opened. In 1913, it was renamed the Orpheum Theatre, and it showed movies until it closed in 1929.

In 1931, it reopened as a movie house and was renamed the Roxy Theatre, but by 1933, new owner George Young turned it into a nationally-known house of burlesque.

In a 1977 newspaper article, Young recalled, "During my day, the Roxy grossed $7,000 a week and was a real moneymaker. Lou Gehrig, as clean living a man as you'd ever meet, got a great kick out of the comics and never missed a visit to the Roxy when the New York Yankees were in town. He'd never accept a free pass, just wanted to sit in the last row and laugh. Joe DiMaggio was also a great fan of the Roxy comics."

Throughout its heyday, the Roxy Theatre was a stopover for entertainers such as Abbott & Costello, Phil Silvers, Red Buttons, Ann Corio, and Tempest Storm. The Roxy Theatre became the best-known burlesque house in Cleveland, attracting major touring burlesque acts and achieving a national reputation.

Roxy Theatre in Cleveland, Ohio.
PHOTO COURTESY OF: LEE STUART.

In 1956, new owners Frank Engel and Frank Bryan remodeled the theatre and brought their Eastern Burlesque Circuit to Cleveland. At that time, headliners were Rose La Rose and Blaze Starr. From 1968, the Roxy Theatre alternated between live entertainment and X-rated movies. In 1971, the theatre and property were sold to Kope Reality for $150,000. It became necessary to break both the 1906 lease agreement and Swetland's will, which had stipulated that after his death, the property should be continuously leased and the income divided between Oberlin College and Western Reserve College, then part of Case Western Reserve University. With approval from the remaining heirs, the $150,000 sale price was evenly split between the two institutions.

In September 1972, the lobby of the Roxy Theatre was bombed, but in February 1973, the theatre reopened showing X-rated films. In November 1977, the Roxy Theatre closed permanently. The National City Bank bought the property and tore down the theatre to make room for the National City Center.

GAYETY THEATRE
COLUMBUS, OHIO

During 1915-1916, the Knickerbocker Theatre was built at 246-54 South High Street. The impressive façade had three arched bays of multi-colored terra cotta that were separated by rectangular columns and topped with realistic lion heads. The theatre operated as a venue for vaudeville shows and motion pictures.

In the 1940s and 1950s, it was renamed the Gayety Theatre and became a burlesque house. In the late 1950s, the theatre closed. In 1960, its auditorium was torn down to make way for a parking lot. During the 1970s, various businesses continued to operate from the former lobby space and upstairs offices. In 1980, the remaining Gayety Theatre structure, along with its still-elegant terra cotta façade, was demolished as part of the city's urban renewal plan.

Additional Burlesque Theatres that need mentioning include:

MINSKY'S ADAMS THEATRE, NEWARK, NEW JERSEY
THE ALVIN, MINNEAPOLIS, MINNESOTA
THE AVENUE, DETROIT, MICHIGAN

The Capitol, Portland, Oregon
The Casino, Boston, Massachusetts
The Casino, Pittsburgh, Pennsylvania
The Embassy, Rochester, New York
The Empire, Toledo, Ohio
The Empress, Detroit, Michigan
The Empress, Milwaukee, Wisconsin
The Esquire, Toledo, Ohio
The Gaiety, Norfolk, Virginia
The Gem Follies, Chicago, Illinois
The Fox, Indianapolis, Indiana
The Globe, Atlantic City, New Jersey
The Grand, Canton, Ohio
The Grand, Youngstown, Ohio
The Hollywood, San Diego, California
The Old Howard, Boston, Massachusetts
The Irving Place, New York, New York
The Lyceum, Columbus, Ohio
The Lyric, Allentown, Pennsylvania
The Lyric, Philadelphia, Pennsylvania
The Mayfair, Dayton, Ohio
The National, Louisville, Kentucky
The National Winter Garden, New York, New York
The Palace, Buffalo, New York
The Palace, Youngstown, Ohio
The Rivoli, Seattle, Washington
The Savoy, Louisville, Kentucky
The Star, Portland, Oregon
The State, Canton, Ohio
The Third Avenue, Portland, Oregon
The Tivoli, Denver, Colorado
The Town Hall, Toledo, Ohio
The Troc, Philadelphia, Pennsylvania
The World, St. Louis, Missouri
The Majestic, Madison, Wisconsin
The Riverside, Milwaukee, Wisconsin

There were also Gayety Theatres and Gaiety Theatres all across the country.

Hollywood Burlesque Theatre in San Diego, California.
PHOTO COURTESY OF: LARRY KANE.

On stage at the Hollywood Burlesque Theatre, in San Diego, California, 1943. Front row, third from the right, Frances Johnston.
PHOTO COURTESY OF: DEE ANN JOHNSTON-COMBES.

Ticket from the National Winter Gardens Theatre.
PHOTO COURTESY OF: BURLESQUE HISTORICAL SOCIETY.

Rivoli Theatre marquee, Seattle, Washington.
PHOTO COURTESY OF: LEE STUART.

Rivoli Theatre building, Seattle, Washington.
PHOTO COURTESY OF: LEE STUART.

Star Theatre marquee, Portland, Oregon.
PHOTO COURTESY OF: LEE STUART.

The front of the Star Theatre in Portland, Oregon.
PHOTO COURTESY OF: LEE STUART.

Town Hall Burlesque Theatre front, Toledo, Ohio.
PHOTO COURTESY OF: BURLESQUE HISTORICAL SOCIETY.

**Troc Burlesque Theatre,
Philadelphia, Pennsylvania.**
PHOTO COURTESY OF: MARA GAYE
& THE SIEGFRIED FAMILY.

**Gayety Burlesque
Theatre, Toledo, Ohio.**
PHOTO COURTESY OF:
LEE STUART.

The musicians from the Gayety Theatre in Toledo, Ohio.
PHOTO COURTESY OF: LEE STUART.

Gaiety Burlesque Theatre, Oklahoma City, Oklahoma.
PHOTO COURTESY OF: LEE STUART.

Old-time burlesque theatre chorus line.
PHOTO COURTESY OF: LEE STUART.

Old-time burlesque theatre chorus line.
PHOTO COURTESY OF: LEE STUART.

Old-time burlesque theatre chorus line.
PHOTO COURTESY OF: LEE STUART.

Old-time burlesque performer relaxing backstage.
PHOTO COURTESY OF: LEE STUART.

Old-time burlesque theatre chorus line.
PHOTO COURTESY OF: LEE STUART.

Finale from an old-time burlesque show.
PHOTO COURTESY OF: BURLESQUE HISTORICAL SOCIETY.

Some Carnival History, Too!

There were a number of burlesque and vaudeville performers working in carnivals over the years, especially when theatres closed down during the summer months. During the 1930s, girl revues were created. These production-type shows consisted of eight-piece and ten-piece stage bands, eight to twelve girls in a chorus line, four to five exotic or fan dancers, a couple of vaudeville acts or specialty numbers, with a comic or two thrown in.

After World War Two, the big carnivals still carried this type of revue. In 1946, burlesque stars began regularly appearing in the carnival girl shows. Gypsy Rose Lee, Sally Rand, and Georgia Sothern were probably the highest-paid features any carnival carried. They drew more than enough patronage to pay their salaries and show a profit for the midway. The advent of the spectacular rides in the 1950s and 1960s doomed big theatre type shows on carnival midways.

Sally Rand, perhaps the most well-known of these performers, was hired for $1,000 a week to perform at the 1933 Century of Progress at the Chicago World's Fair, where her fan dance made her a household name. Rand was arrested the first night at the fair and charged with indecent exposure. From that point on, her career blossomed.

In 1939, Rand's *Miss America 1939* girl show, part of the Golden Gate Exposition, grossed $44,000 and drew 175,000 customers. In 1947, Sally's show was the feature attraction on the *Hennies Brothers Show*. At the Iowa State Fair in Des Moines, her show reported a net gross of over $9,000 after taxes. Over the course of one week, that show brought in $40,000. Only a few years before, an entire carnival midway was lucky to gross that much in a year's time. Sally Rand was earning that amount in one week.

In 1948, Sally worked in the Royal American Show *Girl Revue*. Her show consisted of twelve chorus girls, two dance teams, three comics, an organist, and Sally. It attracted more than 500,000 customers. In 1949, the Royal American Show hired Gypsy Rose Lee as their feature. Gypsy did almost as well as Sally had done in 1948; the difference was only due to the price of the tickets. It cost $1 to see Sally and 75¢ cents to see Gypsy.

In 1950, Rand appeared with Al Wagner's *Cavalcade of Amusement*. Her show was called *The Royal American Girl Revue*. In January 1951, Wagner filed a lawsuit against Sally and NBC for $2 million, stating that Sally made a comment, which NBC broadcast, saying he owed her $23,000. Wagner said this comment "hurt his reputation." He lost the case, and the court settlement cost Wagner $10,514. Throughout the 1950s, Sally continued working carnival shows, mainly with the Cetlin & Wilson Fairs. She liked carnival life and the "carnies" all liked her. In 1958, Sally Rand performed her last season under the canvas.

Faith Bacon, on the other hand, was unpopular on the carnival circuit. In 1948, John R. Ward built a new show for Faith and spent a great deal of time fighting with her. In early June, she sued Ward and his show for $5,044, which she claimed he owed her. There was a definite personality conflict between the two. Ward alleged that Faith broke her contract by not working at specific times in shows required by their contract. Faith countered that he would not allow her to work and that either he or some of his employees had thrown handfuls of tacks on stage in front of her as she attempted to perform her "Dance of the Veils" number barefooted. Faith soon left the show—most likely without the money she claimed Ward owed her.

Georgia Sothern's encounter with the carnival world is another story. Georgia, a headliner at Minsky's in New York City, entered the carnival world by signing a contract with the James E. Strates Shows to tour for thirty weeks in 1948. She was so popular that the management charged 65¢ admission just to watch her rehearse before the show actually opened in Washington, D.C.

Performers from burlesque were the carnival fad, particularly from the late 1940s throughout the 1950s. Besides those already mentioned, performers who worked the carnivals included Evelyn West, who drew record crowds in 1951; Carrie Finnell in 1948; Zorita, who was featured in the *World of Mirth Show* in 1950; Jennie Lee, who worked Canadian carnivals in 1954 and 1956; and specialty dancer Mimi Reed, who worked the *Royal American's Girl Show* in 1959.

Comics also worked carnivals. Al Anger, Harry Savoy, Art Watts, Benny "Wop" Moore, and Billy Reed became a fixture over the years in carnival revue shows. They never failed to draw big crowds, but the girls from old-time burlesque drew the biggest crowds. Other dancers working the midways included Barbara Curtis, Mitzi, Val Valentine, Bonnie Boyia, Darlene Drake, Pagan Jones, Crystal Ames, Blaze Fury, Ricki Covette, Betty "Blue Eyes" Howard, Tirza, Jessica Rogers, Yvette Dare, Ann Perri, Zorima, Rita Cortez, Sabrina, Bunny Ware, Gale Winds, Denise Darnell, Peggy Reynolds, Mona Vaughn, and Siska and her MacCaw, a parrot named "Pete."

All this began with "Little Egypt." There are no records showing that girl shows or revues existed in the outdoor amusement field or in tent shows prior to the Columbian Exposition. Dancers from the Far East were not "wild," as it was first reported. Seeing those dancers perform using various muscle controls was a new experience for Americans visiting the fair. It is doubtful that any woman calling herself "Little Egypt" appeared on the fairgrounds in Chicago in 1893. However, "cooch" dancing done in the small tents off the fairgrounds is where the legend of "Little Egypt" really began.

When the Columbian Exposition of 1893 was over, most street promoters promised their patrons they would provide them with "Little Egypt" in a "Streets of Cairo" show direct from the World's Fair. In those early shows, the "cooch" dancers were only a small part of the show. Jugglers, glassblowers, gun-spinners, and a variety of Middle-Eastern entertainers worked along with the dancing girls. All the big carnivals carried a "Streets of Cairo" show until the early teens, when different types of shows began taking over, but the "cooch" dancers remained popular. By 1915, some midway owners were experimenting with tented theatres in which they presented dancing girl revues similar to the ones that became popular later on.

Fahreda Mahzar, the real "Little Egypt," was born in Syria around 1872. She was a dancer in "A Street in Cairo" at the 1893 Columbian Exposition in Chicago, and she was the most talked-about entertainer. The price of a ticket to see her perform cost as much as 70¢, while other acts charged only 25¢. At that exorbitant price, "Little Egypt" sold out her shows.

The *New York Herald-Tribune* wrote, "She drew more attention than the seventy-ton telescope or the six-block-long Manufactures and Liberal Arts Building."

Mahzar, who claimed to be the originator of the "muscle dance" in America, was entitled to be called the original "Little Egypt." It is believed that she never actually danced on the exposition fairgrounds, but worked in a small tent show outside the fairgrounds. At that time, Mahzar did have documented proof that she originated the dance that helped make the 1893 Columbian Exposition a success. She was credited with being the original "Little Egypt."

In 1905, Mahzar married Andrew Spyrpoulos, a Chicago restaurant owner. In 1933, her last public appearance was made at the Chicago Century of Progress, billed as the "Queen of the Midway." On April 5, 1937, she died in Chicago and was buried in Elmhurst, Illinois.

Sally Rand.
PHOTO COURTESY OF: BURLESQUE HISTORICAL SOCIETY.

Carnival fronts of the Hennies Bros Girl Show in Springfield, Illinois; August 1946.
PHOTOS COURTESY OF: BURLESQUE HISTORICAL SOCIETY.

Carrie Finnell.
PHOTO COURTESY OF: BURLESQUE
HISTORICAL SOCIETY.

BELOW:
Jennie Lee with new friend.
PHOTO COURTESY OF: PAT FLANNERY.

BELOW RIGHT:
Jennie Lee.
PHOTO COURTESY OF: PAT FLANNERY.

Barbara Curtis.
PHOTO COURTESY OF: AL BAKER JR.

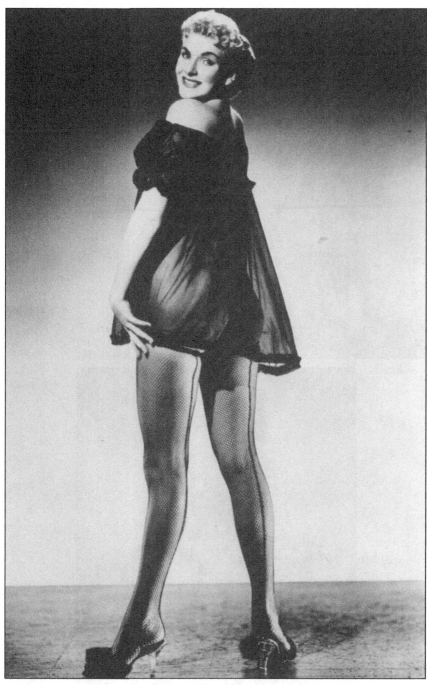

Ricki Covette.
PHOTO COURTESY OF: AL BAKER JR.

Jessica Rogers.
PHOTO COURTESY OF:
MARINKA.

BELOW:
Ann Perri.
PHOTO COURTESY OF:
AL BAKER JR.

RIGHT:
Denise Darnell.
PHOTO COURTESY OF: IRVING BENSON.

BELOW:
Mona Vaughn.
PHOTO COURTESY OF: MONA
VAUGHN/BURLESQUE HISTORICAL
SOCIETY.

The Burlesque Industry of Today

In 2001, when www.burlesquehistory.com was posted on the Internet, I received e-mails from some young strippers asking if they could link their sites to ours. At that time, I did not like what I saw and said no thanks. The Golden Days of Burlesque Historical Society is a historical society. Recently, I have been in touch with a few young dancers, looked at their web sites or read about their work, and realized just how interested some of the young dancers are in old-time burlesque. These are women like many other dancers out there, and they cherish the history. They have invested in costumes and have put together appropriate music for the theatrical routines they perform. I feel there is a difference between those working in everyday strip clubs and those performing in Neo-Burlesque. If the history is going to be preserved, it will be up to young women like these to do so. I know there are many performing old-style burlesque, but I would like to introduce you to a just a few performing in the burlesque industry of today. The four who have contributed to this chapter have been fun to communicate with. They have also taught me a lot about the burlesque industry of today.

Since 1992, I have solely been involved with old-time burlesque and its performers. When I decided to add this chapter, I sent these gals a list of questions and challenged them to open my mind regarding the burlesque performers of today. They have done a good job, and their stories are told in their own words.

MISS RAVENNA BLACK

"My mother started me in tap and ballet classes at the age of three, piano lessons at five, and I studied the performing arts throughout my childhood. I became interested in musical theatre as a pre-teen, and attended a special high school for the arts. I didn't see my first burlesque show until 2004, but as soon as I did, I fell in love. My debut burlesque performance was on August 18th, 2005."

"I actually never intended 'Ravenna Black' to be a stage name. It was originally an alias for my work as a pin-up model, but I kept it when I began in burlesque because it truly represented my alter-ego. Each element has a very personal reference: from my "spirit animal," the raven, to a city in Northern Italy. My family is from Southern Switzerland, the Italian-speaking part. I use the AC/DC song, "Back in Black," as a reference to my overcoming the debilitating health problem of morbid obesity. I have about sixteen fully developed acts at the moment, but I'm always thinking up more."

"I work with several costume designers and seamstresses. Some costumes pieces I make myself, like head-dresses and accessories. I have also been known to construct special props. Many of my costumes are vintage dresses that I have added on to and altered to fit my specifications."

"I'm particularly fond of blues songs, and I'm best-known for being comedic and theatrical, using lots of crazy props. My best known numbers are a little Swiss milk maid routine performed to "Keep on Churnin' til the Butter Comes" by Wynonie Harris; a lip-sync routine to the "Pizza" by novelty/cabaret singer Ruth Wallis; and my pirate number, which is performed to the theme song from "Muppet Treasure Island" and ends with a bang from two pyrotechnic flintlock pistols that shoot flame and smoke. I can also twirl tassels, and I am working on a fan dance."

"I have studied anything and everything I could find on the burlesque dancers of yesteryear, both for inspiration and for ideas. I do not pattern myself after anyone in particular, although I do have my favorites. Dee Milo is my all-time favorite. My style is very theatrical; I love to tell a story, and rely heavily on the lyrics in my music. When I saw Dee perform and talked to her about how she used music to tell her story, I knew I had met a kindred spirit. Not only is she beautiful and inspiring artistically, she has given me personal encouragement for which I will always be grateful. Other favorites include Dixie Evans, with her theatrical "Producer" routine; Holiday O'Hara, and her comical "fabric phallus" trick; high-energy Satan's Angel and her fire tassels; and fellow intelligent ecdysiast and Seattle girl, Gypsy Rose Lee."

"I don't know of many burlesque performers who can make a living performing these days. For most of us, burlesque is a labor of love and quite simply, our art. Most Neo-Burlesque shows are in small clubs, although I have had the opportunity to perform in front of some pretty big crowds, as well. I performed for more than 1,000 at a large club in San Francisco, and more than 2,500 at Viva Las Vegas. I perform primarily in Seattle, but I do tour up and down the West coast on a regular basis, performing several times per year in San Francisco and Los Angeles. I get to New York once or twice a year, recently performed in Alaska, and I've worked in Canada. Most of my gigs are in the Seattle area, and I manage to keep quite busy. I have sometimes had as many as nine shows per month, although my overall average since I started has been five shows per month."

"I am nostalgic for the old days of the burlesque theatre. While I enjoy my club gigs, there is nothing quite like a big spotlight on a red velvet curtain. I would like to bring the old-time burlesque show back to the mainstream, first on television as a Benny Hill-meets-The Muppets variety show to introduce modern audiences to the genre, and then once they get it, as a traveling theatre show."

"Today's clubs don't always understand what dancers need. I have had to change and get ready in broom closets, kitchens, and back offices. If I could change anything about working in clubs, I would make sure they all provided clean, well-lit dressing rooms with full length mirrors. Most club shows are still stage shows with no "mixing" required. Unlike modern-day strippers, burlesque dancers only interact with the audience directly when they choose to do so. If I sit in someone's lap or assault someone with my feather boa, he or she is usually giggling or embarrassed, which is why I do it. Someday, I would love to teach future dancers, if they felt I had anything to teach them."

Miss Ravenna Black. Photographer: John Moore, Innovative Images.
PHOTO COURTESY OF: MISS RAVENNA BLACK.

Miss Ravenna Black performing live. Photographer: Paul O'Connell.
PHOTO COURTESY OF: MISS RAVENNA BLACK.

Miss Ravenna Black performing live. Photographer: Paul O'Connell.
PHOTO COURTESY OF: MISS RAVENNA BLACK.

Miss Ravenna Black. Photographer: RJB Photo (Rob Butler).
PHOTO COURTESY OF: MISS RAVENNA BLACK. AUTHORS COLLECTION.

MISS ORCHID MEI

"In 2002, I saw a burlesque show. In 2004, I started dancing, and I knew that's what I was meant to do. It took me quite some time to come up with my moniker. I wanted something that embodied all that I was and wanted to become. I ended up with "Mei Lan Hua," which means "beautiful orchid," because I felt that orchids are not only quintessential beauty, but are also beautifully erotic and exotic. My persona came from within; it's me, the me that I've always known, but suppressed because I was expected to be someone else. I've always performed as "Miss Orchid Mei."

"I have several routines I do that are smaller bits that I've either done once or keep in a random rotation so that neither the audience nor I get bored. I have only a handful of 'signature pieces' that I perform at larger events. The costumes I wear are all vintage inspired, yet they are of my own design. I've used vintage patterns and pictures mixed with my vision of glamour and couture; they are sewn and created by my dearest friend and fellow performer Kitty Crimson and I. I do all of the individual rhinestone work myself."

"I try to stay true to the tradition of old-time burlesque; and in doing so, I watch as many of the old reels and videos I can find and learn from them. I don't have a sole performer that I pattern myself after; I model myself after all of them."

Orchid Mei has performed mostly on the West coast and in Canada. Recently, in early 2009, she appeared on stage in London. She wrote, "I do have a normal job as an Executive Assistant to the President of a company and I have a degree in Chinese language. One day I hope I'll be able to focus on performing. Currently I perform two to four nights a week. I like to perform as much as possible. There really aren't yet many shows here in Denver, but we're working on it. I hope to dance and perform as long as I possibly can. I like to perform to slower music with heavy horns and big introductions. I like dynamics and drama, jazz, blues, classic, and big band. If I'm moved by the song, I feel I will create something that will move the audience, as well. I can twirl tassels, but I don't often do so. However, I do work with fans; I love them. I use traditional ostrich fans, Chinese short fans, and Chinese long-ribbon fans. Eventually, I'll work in traditional Korean fans, too. I'm sure that I'll eventually teach; the tradition must live on, and through that is education."

"I love old-time burlesque's suggestiveness, the symbolism, theatrics, showmanship, costuming, and especially that the performers remained every bit a lady, even though they were comparable to rock stars of today. I would love to perform in more theatres, especially the older ones; they are so beautiful. Convincing someone of something isn't an easy task, especially if you are attempting to emulate and honor them. You can't really tell the legends from burlesque that you may be like them in any way; they have to feel it. I would have to get over my shyness and speak in-depth with them; I would also love to perform for them."

Miss Orchid Mei. Photographer: Mel Haynes.
Courtesy Miss Orchid Mei. Authors Collection.

Miss Orchid Mei. Photographer: Mel Haynes.
PHOTO COURTESY OF: MISS ORCHID MEI.

Miss Orchid Mei. Photographer: Mel Haynes.
PHOTO COURTESY OF: MISS ORCHID MEI.

Miss Kitty Baby

"My burlesque debut came in December 2005. A friend had been egging me on to take an interest in performing for most of the year. Due to my job, I didn't think I should take that step. I worked at sea for eight months of the year and felt that I couldn't perform without more of a presence in the artistic community. My friends put on their annual Toys for Tots fundraiser to collect toys for children at Christmas; normally they had a band, Santa, and raffled prizes. I thought it would increase attendance to throw in a few burlesque numbers and be fun to do for the charity. A girlfriend, the one who pursued me to dance, and I both performed a single routine. Attendance was up compared to previous events, and the fundraiser did very well. Shortly thereafter, I returned to my job at sea."

"Three months later when I hit land again, I was invited to perform in a dance troupe. It was agreed that my attendance depended on when I would be home from my job at sea. Besides paid shows, I have donated my talents and performing skills to many charity shows and fundraisers."

"A coworker on my fishing boat gave me the name 'Kitty Baby' after everyone simply called me 'Kitty' for over five years. The addition of the 'Miss' in 'Miss Kitty Baby' is used to create a better rhythm and flow for stage presentation and makes it easier on the Master of Ceremonies. In the spring of 2006, I developed a presence on MySpace.com and worked as a pin-up model. I also took to the burlesque stage for real."

"I'm a very intense person, and I know this translates to the stage. I am known for my high-energy, shimmy number and the ability to give until it hurts. I'm a former United States Marine, and I spent ten years as an Alaskan fisherman. Although I haven't normally used this to describe myself, it is a favorite for the Master of Ceremonies. I have even had a Master of Ceremonies change my pre-written introduction to one of their liking that included my military service. Believe it or not, I don't have a kitten or kitty number; and I have not yet done a pin-up photo shoot with that theme either. So far, I have only used the stage name 'Miss Kitty Baby,' but I do have an alter ego comedy name as a backup if I ever need it: 'Penelope Van Der Bump.'"

"I have nine routines that I perform. In the works, I have several more for which I have purchased costume materials and chosen music. These are works-in-progress and they are nice to have for continuous creativity. I make all of my own costumes; I love the costumes."

"I take inspiration from the general world of vintage burlesque. I have many different DVDs containing old footage, as well as a few great books showcasing the performers and their costumes. I started as a contemporary performer because my only influence was the modern performers I had seen. I very quickly started my DVD and book collection to basically self-teach. Of course, I was fascinated and impressed; I fell in love with the styles and the costumes of vintage burlesque. I started adopting certain costume elements from what I saw. I also began incorporating certain moves, choreography, order, and flow from the old acts. I am so inspired by vintage burlesque that it is my mission to bring it to the modern stage as much as I can. In the old days of burlesque shows, the audience was happy enough to see a nearly naked body, or so I imagine. Today, they expect a bit more theatrics, but I know I can achieve my goal."

"I perform an act that is a recreation of a vintage act. The costume and choreography are nearly exact. The music is different, but it fits the original dance moves just right. I bill this act as "A Vintage Burlesque Act Originally Performed by Mary Blair." I will not step foot on stage unless this is announced. I was so inspired by this little number because it seemed so contemporary and daring for it's time. It has elements in it that you don't often see today in that the lower region is the final reveal. I love bringing that to the stage."

"I am a regular guest instructor at a burlesque class here in Seattle. One thing I teach is how to research vintage burlesque and learn the history. I provide a list of videos and books, and I explain different costume elements that were unique to the time and why. I encourage the students to learn the history and be inspired by the performance elements of the past. One of these students from the December 2007 class obviously took this to heart, and it has been a pleasure to see what she has come up with."

"I know enough history to know that I am extremely interested in vintage burlesque, but I am no expert. My favorites from old-time burlesque include Jennie Lee for her incredible body and ability to perform with such intensity and confidence. Her performance in 'Sleepy Time Gal' simply blows me away. To the untrained eye it could look like just another burlesque number; to me, she has moves and confidence that most modern performers I have seen can't even come close to."

"Another favorite of mine is Lili St Cyr. Although I am not partial to blondes, she is one of the most beautiful creatures I have ever laid eyes on. Some of this may have to do with the fact that the old footage of her is in very warm colors. I am mesmerized by her beauty. She was also very forward-moving in creating her own niche to define her in the artistic world. I have always been impressed by that."

"Patti Waggin is another favorite of mine because of her ability to dance and shimmy for what seems like forever, just never stopping. She makes me so happy, like a kid at Christmas. I have even taken a few little steps of hers and thrown them into routines of mine. No one will probably ever notice, but I know in my heart that this is paying homage to her skills."

"I appreciate Gypsy Rose Lee for sharing her life with us through her autobiography. She helps us not only understand her life and what it was like to enter and influence the world of burlesque."

"Vicky Lynn performs the most impressive and courageous Boy-lesque/drag act I have ever seen. His/Her moves were perfect for a very feminine performer and were more 'spot on' than some modern female dancers, which was very contemporary for the time."

"All the women of color and mixed race who performed on the burlesque stage and in the old videos really have my respect. I know that burlesque was a 'blue art' to begin with, and at a time of segregation, it must have taken a lot of guts and determination to be part of the burlesque world. I may be way off base because I didn't live during that time, but this is my best guess. I enjoy seeing these beautiful women along with all the other beauties."

"I perform primarily in Seattle and California, but I have worked all over the West coast, as well as in Arizona, Colorado, Las Vegas, and in Canada. I absolutely love working in theatres, but it's not easy to get many shows in theatres."

"There are some really nice stages in some clubs and the seating is arranged in a way for a burlesque show that you can dance on the floor if you have a follow spotlight. This is fun for the audience because you can give them a chance to get a little bit closer to you and interact with you, depending on the act. Then, you can perform the rest of your act on the stage. The combined Rock n' Roll and Burlesque show has it's time and place, but it's often difficult to get the stage clear enough to perform your routines, which is my personal pet peeve."

"In the shows I work, you don't have to mix with the audience, but it can be really fun for you and a real treat for them, as well. I like having a prop to share with them, doing a dance routine among the tables, having a specific clothing item I need help with, honoring a birthday or a bride-to-be, and making a floor entrance."

"I have had some not-so-great experiences in clubs. Once, when I stepped out from the curtain to see that the audience members were off to the sides, and nothing but cameras were in front of me. There should have been some crowd control. My act was very specific, and because of the seating arrangements, I was not performing for the audience, but the cameras instead. To this day, I have not seen one photograph from that night. Having a drunken man decide to 'dance' with me on stage and not be handled by security in a timely manner was not fun. I have also had occasions when I had trouble getting steps to the stage, getting the stage cleared of microphone stands and cords, and getting music in the monitors so I can hear it on stage."

"My first numbers were to songs that I loved: rockabilly songs and a soundtrack song from a favorite movie. I mostly perform to rockabilly music, as I am a 'Rockabilly Gal' and it inspires me the most. For instrumentals or second songs, I really like 'Exotica' and Las Vegas grind style music from the late 1950s and early 1960s. Recently, I have found a radio station that plays nothing but music from the 1940s and 1950s, including a lot of swing and big band, but no rock n' roll. This has been so inspirational for me; it seems that I am writing down a new song title every other day to which I want to dance."

"I don't have any specific routines, but I am well-known for my 'Zombie Hula' number and my 'Baby Blue' number that won second place at the Viva Las Vegas Burlesque competition in my first year as a performer. I do twirl tassels, and I make all of my own pasties.

I have not worked with large fans yet. I would like to, but I still feel I'm a complete performer even if I don't work with fans. I already teach as a guest instructor at Trixie Lane's Kindergarten of Burlesque, which can be explored further at www.burlesqueclass.com."

"I have a passionate love for burlesque; I love the costumes, music, history, and the formula that makes a burlesque act and show, as well as audience teasing. I love celebrating the female body in a suggestive yet very controlled way. I love entertaining the audience with my energy, and I love that I can share this with my audience, yet I can still dress after my show and return to the crowd a classy lady sharing a cocktail with my fans that love and respect the show."

"Be aware, I am heavily tattooed. I began getting tattoos fifteen years ago in 1993. I have only been performing burlesque for a couple of years. I will completely understand if this is too much for the women from old-time burlesque to deal with, but my tattoos are very important to me and I am quite proud of them. They help define who I am as a person. Aside from the tattoos, I love all things vintage. I have a huge collection of clothes, dresses, purses, shoes, jewelry, and furs from the 1940s, 1950s, and 1960s. My beautiful art deco condo was built in 1929 and is filled with furniture from those decades, so you can see that I am in love with mid-century culture."

One final note regarding Miss Kitty Baby, something she didn't know I would mention. She and several other young women were involved in a creation of a wonderful 2009 pin-up calendar. The photos were all shot aboard the Queen Mary, the ladies all wore vintage clothing, and the sales benefit our soldiers. I hope you will support their efforts, now, and in the future.

Jane,
Thanks for
Everything! ♡
Love Always,
Kitty
Baby

Miss Kitty Baby. Photographer: RJB Photo (Rob Butler).
PHOTO COURTESY OF: MISS KITTY BABY. AUTHORS COLLECTION.

Miss Kitty Baby. Photographer: RJB Photo (Rob Butler).
Photo courtesy of: Miss Kitty Baby.

Miss Kitty Baby.
Photographer: RJB Photo
(Rob Butler).

AVA GARTER

"I first started dancing as a go-go dancer when I was sixteen years old in nightclubs in Southern California. I used a fake ID and made my way into the club, or I went to teen night clubs in my town. I really enjoyed dancing and wished that I had taken lessons in ballet, jazz, or tap when I was younger, but I knew that it would have been too expensive. Dance class consisted of not just the fee for the actual classes, but the costumes and the shoes necessary for the performances. My mom was a single mother of two girls, and dance lessons would have been just too much for her to afford. I never asked or even mentioned it"

"I call myself a 'burlesque entertainer.' I really don't pay attention to what the proper names are. My stage name came about when I was sitting at friend Dita Von Teese's house. Three of us were discussing my respect and admiration for the beautiful movie star, Ava Gardner. We decided that a great burlesque name should always have a good playful wink in it, and we all thought Ava Garter was a perfect stage name."

"Many years ago, when I worked in a gentleman's club, I danced by the name "Mina." I was a huge fan of Bram Stoker's *Dracula* and loved the character of Mina. I was actually obsessed with it for a while, embarrassingly enough. I couldn't get enough of watching the movie and I watched it over and over again. When the time came for me to come up with a name, I simply used what I loved."

"My friends and mentors, Dita Von Teese, Catherine D'Lish, and I have all spent years performing in gentlemen's clubs. For me, I feel that performing in those clubs for years has made me a smoother, sexier, and more confident, dancer. My club experience has made it easy for me to have direct eye contact when I perform, or when I am in front of a camera."

"While working in clubs, I met girls that were putting themselves through law school, single mothers that had left abusive husbands and were supporting themselves alone with no help from the state, single girls doing all right on their own, and independent women who were smart and happy. Yes, some were miserable and on drugs, but those were the ones that I avoided. I used the experience to propel myself to a higher level in life, and I feel the relationships made me a better person. It is very easy for people on the outside to judge women, when they haven't spent the time I have with them. With all due respect, I don't want to offend anyone, but I have never been a nude dancer. I have always remained a classy and upscale performer in every club or theatre I worked. However, I will never judge other women for whatever choices they made for themselves or for their families. Sometimes, people have to do what they have to do. I feel that if I point fingers, three others point back at me. I believe burlesque is a form of theatrical art, where as strip club dancing is just fun entertainment aimed mostly at men."

"I have six solid acts. I have three costumes that were made by Catherine D'Lish; the rest are made by me with the help of my friends at Trashy Lingerie in Beverly Hills, California. I perform regularly on Friday and Saturday nights at the Queen Mary. It is a great place in which to perform burlesque shows. I am the only girl who really takes anything off, so I get most of the attention. The girl wearing the fewest clothes wins. I perform anywhere from three to five nights a week. I am not a tassel twirler; it's just not my style. I prance and glide, work with fans, furs, tons of rhinestones in every act, and I always glitter. The more sparkle, the better. Someday, I would love to teach and I can also see myself making costumes. I don't perform to modern music; I find classic burlesque music is best for my style."

"There are many different women from old-time burlesque that I find inspirational. I love Sally Rand's story of going from chorus girl to superstar. Most of the women that we all love have a common thread in their story: they needed to survive and they happened upon our fantastic career. They all kind of fell into it because of a need; none really grew up saying, 'Hey, I want to do that!' I admire all the women from burlesque that had the courage to go out on a stage and do a job that was politically incorrect and socially unacceptable as a viable job for a lady. They were all brave, and because of that, they are all heroines to me. I would very much like to learn more about the women of burlesque from days gone by. I think that it is something that I need to do."

"I love working in theatres; it's such a thrill. It is truly where burlesque should be performed. I also like that the performers and people involved in old-time burlesque were original creators that came up with funny and unique names and routines. I miss vaudeville.

Routines like 'Who's on First?' are really missing in the shows performed these days."

"As for working in clubs and bars, what frustrates me most is the lack of lighting. I can give the best show of my life, but it does not matter if the audience can't see it. Some of the clubs are very ill-equipped to handle the shows we bring them. The other problem seems to be the type of stages provided for the shows. Often, they are on the same level as the audience, when they should be raised above them. I perform this way most every weekend, so I am used to it, but it allows audience members to reach out, try to touch me, and attempt to get into my act, which I have experienced more than once."

"When I worked in Japan, I felt that the audiences were so kind. They have an appreciation for production numbers and shows over there that we just haven't yet tapped. Someday soon, I would thoroughly enjoy entertaining them with my current burlesque act. I have also made the decision not to ever again give up being a dancer. I am very unhappy when I don't dance."

"As for convincing women who worked in old-time burlesque that I am like them, I would hope they could see that I carry myself with class and dignity in my shows and that my style of entertainment will always be playful and classic. I choose to call my dancing style sensuality, not sexuality. That would best describe the way I perform. I hope they would like what I have to offer and be proud to welcome me into their community."

**Ava Garter.
Photographer:
Lori Brystan.**
PHOTO COURTESY
OF: AVA GARTER.

Ava Garter. Photographer: Jake Davis.
Photo courtesy of: Ava Garter.

Ava Garter. Photographer: Marco Patino.
PHOTO COURTESY OF: AVA GARTER.

Some of the many dancers succeeding in the Neo-Burlesque shows of today include Miss Jacqueline Hyde, Vienna La Rouge, Inga Ingenue, La Cholita, Kalani Kokonuts, Flame Cynders, Cardinal Cyn, The Flying Fox, the Pontini Sisters, and Trixie Minx. Vivienne VaVoom is not only a dancer performing regularly in *Burlesque As It Was*, but she is also a successful author.

There are also many performance groups. One example is the Twilight Vixen Revue, a troop from the San Francisco area that performs synchronized fan dances and choreographed group numbers. Other groups include the Boston Baby Dolls, and from New Orleans, Bustout Burlesque, and Fleur de Tease, a premiere variety burlesque revue that includes an assortment of entertainers. Young performers like these are what the burlesque industry of today is all about. They not only perform because they love to dance and entertain, but many also work normal day jobs.

Many young performers, and events such as the Boston Burlesque Expo, are working to preserve the history and style of old-time burlesque. Their various talents go into creating costumes, developing routines, teaching, and sometimes even producing shows. If you have the chance to see them perform, or go to an event, please take the opportunity and support them. Check out their web sites for performance schedules.

Books of Choice

I have studied burlesque for many years, and due to my interest, I have accumulated quite a library. However, I have not read or gained access to all the books that have been written on burlesque. Only nonfiction books are mentioned in this listing, but these are the books I consider to be some of the best and most informative about old-time burlesque. They are a good place to start if you're just beginning to learn.

Many wonderful books and articles can also be located that may discuss burlesque on only two or three pages, or in one chapter. Earl Wilson, Abel Green, and Joe Laurie, Jr. wrote some great books regarding the entertainment industry of yesteryear. I challenge you to research and find the books you enjoy. Robert Allen included a brilliant bibliography in his book. I am simply suggesting a few of my personal favorite books, and this list is far from complete.

Anyone wanting to read, study, and collect books about old-time burlesque can start with this list. However, be aware that there are many more out there. For example, I know Erik Lee Preminger and David Kruh have published additional books regarding burlesque. There is a recent release about Lydia Thompson that I have heard is excellent; and Lillian Brown self-published her memoirs in 2003. More books are being published all the time, in fact I just received a copy of a new book on Gypsy Rose Lee, written by Noralee Frankel, and published by Oxford University Press. So read, and enjoy exploring the books you like the best.

Alexander, H. M. *Strip Tease: The Vanished Art of Burlesque.* New York: Knight Publisher, 1938.

Allen, Robert. *Horrible Prettiness: Burlesque and American Culture.* Chapel Hill: University of North Carolina Press, 1986.

Briggeman, Jane. *Burlesque: Legendary Stars of the Stage.* Portland: Collectors Press, 2004.

Bruce, Honey. *Benenson, D. Honey.* Chicago: Playboy Press, 1976.

Collyer, Martin. *Burlesque.* New York: Lancer Books, 1964.

Corio, Ann and J. DiMona. *This Was Burlesque.* New York: Grosset & Dunlap, 1968.

Havoc, June. *Early Havoc.* New York: Simon & Schuster, 1959.

Havoc, June. *More Havoc.* New York: Harper & Row, 1980.

Knox, Holly. *Sally Rand: From Film to Fans.* Bend: Maverick Publications, 1988.

Kotzan, Doris. *My Journey Burlesque: The Way it Was.* Pittsburgh: RoseDog Books, 2005.

Kruh, David. *Always Something Doing: Boston's Infamous Scollay Square.* Boston: Northeastern University Press, 1989, 1999.

Leavitt, Michael B. *Fifty Years in Theatrical Management.* New York: Broadway Publishing Company, 1912.

Lee, Gypsy Rose. *Gypsy: A Memoir.* New York: Harper & Brothers, 1957.

Lewis, Paul. *Queen of the Plaza: A Biography of Adah Isaacs Menken.* New York: Funk & Wagnalls Company, Inc., 1964.

Mankowitz, Wolf. *Mazeppa: The Lives, Loves and Legends of Adah Isaacs Menken.* New York: Stein and Day Publishers, 1982.

Minsky, M. and M. Machlin. *Minsky's Burlesque.* New York: Arbor House, 1986.

Preminger, Erik Lee. *Gypsy & Me: At Home and on the Road With Gypsy Rose Lee.* Canada: Little, Brown and Company, 1984.

Sobel, Bernard. *Burleycue.* New York: Farrar & Rinehart, 1931.

Sobel, Bernard. *A Pictorial History of Burlesque.* New York: Bonanza Books, 1956.

Sothern, Georgia. *Georgia: My Life in Burlesque.* New York: Signet Books, 1972.

Tippins, Sherill. *February House.* New York: Houghton Mifflin, 2005. (The information on Gypsy in this book is fun to read.)

Zeidman, Irving. *The American Burlesque Show.* New York: Hawthorn Books, 1967.

The Golden Days of Burlesque Historical Society

MEMBERS PAST AND PRESENT
(AS OF JANUARY 2009)

Al Baker, Jr.
Alexandra the Great
Amber Mist
Anastasia
Angel Carter
Anne Howe
Ann Pett
April March
Arpege
Athena (#2)
Ava Leigh
Bambi Sr.
Barbara Curtis
Barbara Kemp
Betty Jo Morgan
Betty Rowland
Beverly Roberts
Bic Carrol
Billie Gibson
Brandy Wilde
Camille 2000
Candy Baby
Candy Cotton
Chastidy Jones
Connie McFelia
Connie Mercedes
Cynthiana

Daisy Delite
Danny Morton
Daphne Lake
Darbi Wilde
Darlene Larson
David Hanson
David Kavalin
Dee Ann Johnston
Dee Milo
Delilah Jones
Dena Prince
Denise Daye
Diane De Lys
Dyanne Thorne
Eli Jackson
Ellye O'Connell
Erin Irish
Ernie Oberg
Ezi Ryder
The Fascinating
   Jennifer
Flame
Floyd Vivino
Frankie Ray
Frenchie Favré
Gene Stapleton
Gilbert Miller

Gina Bon Bon
Holly Parks
Honey Standish
Honey Bee Kennedy
Hope Diamond
Irving Benson
Irving Tuman
Jack Cione
Jan La Salle
Jennifer Fox
Joan Arline
Joan McCoy
Joan Torino*
John Mast
Joni Taylor
Julie Taylor
June Harlow
Kalantan
KC Kitty
K. C. Layne
Kiva
Lady Midnight
Laline Francis
La Savona
Laura Lee
Lee Angel
Lee Flowers

Leri Vale
Leroy Griffith
Letha Lynn
Lili Marlene
Lili St. Clair
Lillian Gibson
Lillyann Rose
Linda Doll
Little Egypt
Lois De Fee
Lorraine Lee
Lorraine Terbuggen
Lottie "The Body"
Lynn O'Neill
Mademoiselle
    Chiffon
Marg Connell
Maria Bradley
Marilyn Marzette
Marinka
Mary Ann Bellin
Mary Rooney
Maxine Hayes
Maynard Sloate
Ming Chu
Mink Frost
Miss White Fury
Misty Knyte
Mitzi Doerre
Nocturne
The Norwegian
    Doll
Novita
Olga
Paprika Red
Pat Flannery
Pat Merl
Patti Starr

Patty O'Farrell
Paul De Savino Jr.
Penny Powers
Raven
Ricki Covette
Rikki Simone
Rita Atlanta
Ronnie Bell
Rubberlegs
Ruthie Lewis
Rusty Lane
Sandra Ellis
Sandra Sexton
Sandy O'Hara
Satin Doll
Scotti Joyce*
Sequin
Sheila Rae
Sunny Day
Sunny Lee
Susan Gaye
Susan Mills
Taffey O'Neill
Tagore
Tanya
Tee Tee Red
Teri Starr
Tiffany Diamond
Toni Carroll
Tony Midnite*
Topaz
Tura Satana
Val Valentine
Vicki O'Day
Vivi Lynn
Alma Denny
Ann Corio*
Artie Brooks*

Athena*
Betty Briggs*
Betty Francisco*
Betty Ware*
Bonnie Boyia*
Bronya*
Caprice*
Carmela*
Chuck Diamond*
D. G. Griggs*
Dexter Maitland*
Diana Van Dyne*
Diane Raye*
Doreen Gray*
Dottie O'Day*
Electra*
Eileen Hubert*
Flame Fury*
Flame O'Neil*
Florence Lane*
Francita*
Frankie Capri*
Galatea
Gia Nina*
Gilda*
Gussie Gross*
Grace Reed*
Hedy Jo Starr*
Honey Harlow*
Howard
    Montgomery*
Janne Cafara*
Jeanine France*
Jerry Lucas*
Jezebel*
Jimmy Mathews*
Joey Faye*
Joanne Dimples*

Julie Adorn*
Larry Kane
Lee Stuart*
Leonard Reed*
Liberty West*
Lili St. Cyr*
Linda Leslee*
Mara Gaye*
Margie Hart*
Marvan*
Maylo*
Mickie Dennis*
Mike Gilmore*

Mimi Reed*
Mitzi*
Mona Vaughn*
Norma Jean Watts*
Pat Elliott Minsky*
Peggy Lloyd*
Pepper Powell*
Peter "Sonny"
    Thomas*
Rose Weller*
Sally Marr*
Shawna St. Clair*
Shelley Rae

Sherry Britton*
Stacy Farrell*
Sue Martin*
Sunny Dare*
Sunny Knight*
Tanayo*
Tangerine*
Terry Mixon*
Thareen Auroraa*
Tommy Brice*
Winnie Garrett*
Yvonne Yvette*
Zorita*

*deceased

Frenchie Favré.
Photo courtesy of:
Frenchie Favré.

Beverly Roberts.
PHOTO COURTESY OF: BEVERY ROBERTS.

June Harlow.
PHOTO COURTESY OF: BURLESQUE HISTORICAL SOCIETY.

Hope Diamond.
Photo courtesy of: Burlesque Historical Society.

Hope Diamond.

ABOVE AND RIGHT:
Topaz.
PHOTOS COURTESY OF: TOPAZ.

OPPOSITE LOWER RIGHT:
**Program featuring Topaz at the
Old Howard from April 1946.**
PHOTO COURTESY OF: TOPAZ.

Just Some of the Ladies from Old-Time Burlesque

This is not a complete listing of all those who ever danced on a burlesque stage, nor does it include women who are a part of the Neo-Burlesque scene. Not all of the women on this list were exotic dancers; some were specialty dancers. (Those with an * by their names are or have been associated with The Golden Days of Burlesque Historical Society). I include this list not only to remember some of these ladies, but to show just how many ladies danced in burlesque. This listing barely scratches the surface. It is included mostly for people who are curious and truly interested in old-time burlesque. Readers are invited to contact me if they have additional information they would like to share regarding the ladies of old-time burlesque

Babe Abbott
Jeanne Adair
Peggy Adams
*Julie Adorn
Misty Aires
*Alexandra the Great
Honey Alden
Princess Aloha
Amie Amar
Crystal Ames
*Anastasia
Mary Andes
Renee Andre
Jean Andrews

Angel Baby
*Lee Angel
Louise Angel
Marie Annette
Olga Anton
Ann "Bang Bang" Arbor
Babe Archer
Arlene, "The Oyster Girl"
*Joan Arline, "The Sexquire Girl"
Goldie Armond
Dolores Armstead
*Arpege
Beryl Ash

Flo Ash
*Athena (several)
*Rita Atlanta
Kim August
Aurora
Belle Ayre
Baby Bubbles
Baby Doll (several)
Baby Dumpling, "Queen of
    Shimmy"
Baby Jane
Baby Lulu
Faith Bacon
Lee Bailey
Toni Baldwin
Crystal Ball
Countess Barassy
Honey Bare
Kina Bare
Teddi Bare
Joan Barlow
Candy Barr
Lana Barri, "Queen of Shiver"
Lee Barry
Charletta Bates
Wauneta Bates
Sue Bauer
Sandy Beach
Helen Bedd
Honey Bee
Joan Belger
Belinda
Bonnie Bell
Joan Bell
*Ronnie Bell
Tinker Bell
Virginia "Ding Dong" Bell
Billie Bernard

Susan Bishop
Torchy Blair
May Blondell
Marsha Blue
Wanda Blue
Bomba
*Gina Bon Bon
Renee Boughton
*Bonnie Boyia
*Maria Bradley
Dottie Brennan
Melba Brian
*Betty Briggs
*Sherry Britton
*Bronya
Connie Brooks
Leslie Brooks
Louise Brooks
Susan Brown
Julie Bryan
Irene Burke
Fire Burns
Rita Cadillac
*Janne Cafara
*Camille 2000
Sugar Cane
Caniva, "The Grecian Fireball"
*Caprice
Penny Carlton
*Carmela, "The Sophia Loren
    of Burlesque"
Thelma Carpenter
Kitty Carr
Dottie Carroll
Jean Carroll
Joann Carroll
*Toni Carroll
Tracy Carroll

*Angel Carter
Tiffany Cartier
Nona Carver
Cupcakes Cassidy
Ceegon
Charmaine
Pink Champagne
Sheri Champagne
April Chase
Val Chessy
Lorraine Chevalier
Marie Christie
Christina, "The Bronze
    Goddess"
Lily Christine, "The Cat Woman"
Tina Christine
Ming Chu
Penni Cillin
Claudette, "The Baroness"
Annette Cliff
Collette
Bobbi Collins
Icel Condon
Coquette
Marie Cord
Ann Corio
Ricca Cortez
Rita Cortez
Zaza Cortez
Billie Cotton
*Candy Cotton
*Ricki Covette
Ann Curtis
*Barbara Curtis
Desiree Cyn
Stormy Cyn
Cynthia, "The Silhouette"
*Cynthiana

Daccine
Dagmar
Eleanor Dale
Pepper Daly
Petti Dane
Debra Dante
Delilah Dante
JoAnn Dare
*Sunny Dare, "The Girl with
    the Blue Hair"
Yvette Dare
Bubbles Darlene
June Darlene, "The Blonde
    Cyclone"
Linda Darling
Betty Darnell, "More Bounce
    to the Ounce"
Denise Darnell
Jean Darrow
Peggy Davis, "The Blonde
    Venus"
Vicki "Babe" Davis
Gay Dawn (two)
Lili Dawn
Dolores Dawson
*Sunny Day
April Daye
Jerri Dean
Myrna Dean
Dottie "Dimples" Deane
Ilka De Cava
Nicola Dechert
*Lois de Fee
Dorothy De Haven
Denise Delayne
*Daisy Delight
*Diane De Lys
Gaby DeLyse

Venus De Mars
Dorian Dennis, "Miss French
   Riviera"
*Mickie Dennis
*Alma Denny
Trudy Dering
Maxine DeShon
Val de Val
Snooky Dewitt
Susan Dey
Boobs Diamond
*Hope Diamond
*Tiffany Diamond
Caroline Dillard
*Joanne Dimples
Mae Dix
Angela Dixon
*Mitzi Doerre
Gwen Dolan
*Linda Doll
*The Norwegian Doll
*Satin Doll (several)
Princess Do May
Darlene Drake
Helen "Shake" Drake
Kay Drew
Lotus DuBois
Denise Dunbar
Alma Dunning
Naomi Dusk
Ginger Duval
Zonia Duval
*Ecstacy
Sheer Ecstacy
Marcia Edgington
*Little Egypt
*Electra
*Pat Elliott

Kitty Ellis
*Sandra Ellis
Heather English
Dixie Evans
Fabulous Fanny
Connie Fanslau
*Stacy "Eartha Quake" Farrell
*Frenchie Favre
Marilyn Faye
Feline, "The Cat Girl
FiFi
Carrie Finnell
*Flame
*Pat Flannery
April Flowers
*Lee Flowers
Amy Fong
Nora Ford
Kim Foster
Fanne Fox
*Jennifer Fox
Sigrid Fox
Valerie Fox
*Jeanine France
Francine, "The Queen of
   Syncopation"
Helene Francis
*Laline Francis
*Francita
*Wildcat Frenchie, "The Sadie
   Thompson of New Orleans"
*Mink Frost
Blaze Fury, "The Human Heat
   Wave"
*Flame Fury
*Miss White Fury
*Galatea, "The Statue Brought
   to Life by Love"

Helena Gardner
*Winnie Garrett, "The Flaming Redhead"
Bobbie Gay
Lisa Gay
*Mara Gaye
Gloria Gayle
Mademoiselle Gee Gee
*Gilda
Blaza Glory
Lady Godiva
Dixie Gordon
Grace Gordon
Joyce Gordon
Rita Grable
*Doreen Gray
Jade Green, "The Jewish Lollipop"
Diana Grey
Crazylegs Griffin
Beatrice Hall
Pat "Amber" Halliday
Halloween
Rose Hardaway
*Honey Harlow
*June Harlow
Vivian Harris
Doreen Hart
*Margie Hart
Mildred Hart
*Grace Hathaway
*Maxine Hayes
Shirley Hayes, "The Pussy Cat Girl"
Dorothy Henry
*Heska
Georgia Holden
Anna Holland

Wilma Horner
Betty "Blue Eyes" Howard
*Anne Howe
*Eileen Hubert
Bebe Hughes
Mabel Hunter
Jill Huntley, "Miss Dean of Tease"
Jean Idelle
Irma The Body
Erin Irish
Jada
Janeen
Jasmine, "The Portland Rose"
*The Fascinating Jennifer
Robin Jewell
Jezebel (several)
Mary Johnson
*Bambi Jones
Carol Jones, "The Spider Girl"
*Chastidy Jones
*Delilah Jones
Juanita Jones
Libby Jones
Mickey "Ginger" Jones, "The Wham Wham Girl"
Raven Joy
Joan Joyce
*Scotti Joyce
Justine
*Kalantan
Naja Karamaru
Sally Keith
Scarlet Kelly
*Barbara Kemp
Candy Kent
Florabel Kidwell
Mickey Kidwell

June Kiely
Virginia Kinn, "The White Orchid"
Miss Kismet, "Sophisticate of the Orient"
Cherrie Knight
Gay Knight
Ilona Knight
*Sunny Knight
Velvet Knight
*Misty Knyte
Melanie LeBeau
Beverly La Dell
Venus La Doll
Princess Lahoma
*Daphne Lake
Betty La Marr
Louise La Marr
Lillian La Mont
Margaret La Mont
Beverly Lane, "The Girl in the Moon"
*Florence Lane
Melody Lane
*Rusty Lane, "The Duchess of Disrobe"
Sally Lane
Vicki Lane
Rose La Rose
*Darlene Larson
Donnis La Salle
*La Savona, "The Modern Scheherazade"
Louise Laurie
Stella La Vallee
La Vodis
Boo La Von
Jody Lawrence

Sonia Lawrence
*K.C. Layne
Brandy Lee
Gypsy Rose Lee
Heaven Lee
Imogene Lee
Jennie Lee, "The Bazoom Girl"
*Laura Lee
*Lorraine Lee
*Monica Lee
Ruby Lee
*Sunny Lee
Texas Lee
Melanie LeBeau
Abby Leigh
*Ava Leigh
*Linda Leslie
Dottie Lewis
Nancy Lewis, "The Campus Belle"
*Ruthie Lewis
Liah
Tiger Lil
Princess Livingston
*Lia London
Tana Louise, "Heatwave"
Helen Lovett
Lucy Lucern
*Letha Lynn
*Vivi Lynn
Kitty Lynne, "Cat Girl"
Leslie Lynne
Bobbi Mack
Rosa Mack
Mai-Ling (several)
Molly Manor
Marcella

*April March, "The First Lady of Burlesque"
Flo March
June March
*Marg, "The Irish Mist"
*Marinka
*Lilli Marlene
Kitty Marlowe
*Sally Marr
Maxine Marsh
Rusti Marsh
Tina Marshall
Brandy Martin
Martini Martin
*Sue Martin
Maxine Martine
Zee Zee Martine
*Marvan
Marvelle
Marvene
Jan Marvis, "The Sunshine Girl"
*Marilyn Marzette, "The Calendar Girl"
Nikki Masters
*Maylo
Sandy McGuire
Melba, "Toast of the Town"
*Connie Mercedes
Diana Midnight, "The Queen of New Orleans"
*Lady Midnight
Mikyle
Mila, "The Peeler"
Stella Mills
*Susan Mills
*Dee Milo, "Venus of Dance"
*Amber Mist (two)

*Mitzi
Maddy Mixon
*Terry Mixon
Lola Montez
Silver Moon
*Betty Jo Morgan
Chesty Morgan
Marion Morgan
Joan Myers
Nadine, "The Slow Strippin' Queen"
Nalda
Narda
Nervina
Patti Neverbin, "The Platinum Heatwave"
Corky Newton
Nicolette
*Gia Nina
*Nocturne
Poppy Nolan
*Novita
Nudema
Nudine
*Ellye O'Connell
Bunny O'Day
*Dottie O'Day
*Vicki O'Day
Bubbles O'Dell
Chickie O'Dell
Ione O'Donnell
Flash O'Farrell
*Patty O'Farrell
Mickey O'Hara
*Sandy O'Hara, "The Improper Bostonian"
Scarlet O'Hara
*Olga, "The Russian Bombshell"

Nancy Olson, "The Swedish Doll"

Cupcake O'Mason

*Flame O'Neil, "The Heavenly Body"

*Taffey O'Neil

*Lynn O'Neill, "The Garter Girl"

Dardy Orlando

Luella Owens

Candy Page

Kitty Page

LaWanda Page, "Bronze Goddess of Fire"

Lily Pagen

June Palmer

Vicki Palmer

Pat Paree

Ermaine Parker

Frances Parks

*Miss Holly Parks

Valerie Parks

Geraldine Paulette, "The Bongo Queen"

Ida Peel

Chili Pepper

Ann Perri, "The Jane Russell of Burlesque"

*Ann Pett

Kay Pierce

Platina

*Pepper Powell, "The Girl Who Knows How"

Pat "Babe" Powers

*Penny Powers

Irma Pratt

*Dena Prince

Sheba Queen

Debbie Rae

*Gina Rae

*Sheila Rae

*Shelley Rae

Toni Rave

Rita Ravell, "The Latin American Temptress"

*Diane Raye, "England's Sweetheart of Tease"

Olive Raye

Scarlet Rebel

*Paprika Red

*Tee Tee Red

*Grace Reed

Mae Reed

*Mimi Reed

Rae Reed

Pixie Regan

Rita Revere

Ava "Legs" Rey

Jane Rich

Ruby Richards

Jean Richey, "Queen of the Rollers"

*Beverly Roberts

Bobbie Rogers

Jessica Rogers, "The Wow Girl"

Tootsie Roll

*Mary Rooney

*Lily Ann Rose

Toni Rose

*Betty Rowland

Dian Rowland

Rozell Rowland

Rosita Royce

Busty Russell

Marion Russell

Rusty Russell

Sheila "The Peeler" Ryan
Joan Rydell
June "Red" Ryder
*Ezi Ryder
Sabrina
June St. Clair, "Platinum
    Blonde Disrober"
*Lili St. Clair
*Shawna St. Clair
Taffy St. Clair
*Lili St. Cyr
Sally the Shape
Cheri Sands
Sarita, "The Toledo Tornado"
*Tura Satana
Linda Scott
*Sequin
Shalimar
Dorothy Shannon
Lee Sharon
Heidi "Cookie" Shaw
Betty Shea
Tere Sheehan
Barbara Sheridan
Texas Sheridan
Shiva
*Rikki Simone
Sin-Tana, "The Eurasian
    Beauty"
Siri, "The Dutch Doll"
Anna Marie Siska
Reddi Sloane, "The No No
    Girl"
Stunning Smith, "The Girl
    with the Purple Hair"
Georgia Sothern
Jewel Sothern
*Honey Standish

April Starr
Blaze Starr
Kay Starr
*Patti Starr, "Miss Robust"
Pattie Starr
*Teri Starr
Arlene Stevens
Brandy Stevens
Peggy Stiles
Crystal Storm
Georgia Storm
Sharon Storm
Tempest Storm
Jan Story
Mildred "Peaches" Strange
Elaine Stuart
Dixie Sullivan
Margie Sullivan
*Kim Summers
Mary Sunde
Sharon Sutton
Josie Sylvain
*Tagore
*Princess Tana, "The Persian
    Princess"
*Tanayo, "Costa Rica's Dream
    Girl"
*Tangerine
Tornado Tanja
*Tanya
Evelyn Taylor, "The Kiss Girl"
*Joni Taylor
*Julie Taylor
Opal Taylor
Telstar
*Lorraine Terbuggen
Taffy Terrel, "The Candy Kid
    From Texas"

Theodora
Jan Tiffany
Nita Tindall
Tirza
Tornado Tonja
*Topaz, "The Petty Girl of Burlesque"
*Joan Torino
Sue Travis, "The Tantalizer in Tassels"
Irene Tripp
Helen Troy
Trudine, "The Shimmy Queen"
Rhoda "Dimples" True
Lila Turner, "The Zoom Zoom Girl"
*Smokey Turner
Carmen Valdez
Denise Valdez
*Leri Vale
*Val Valentine
Virginia Valentine
Jan Valery
Valetta
Valkyra
Vampira
*Diana Van Dyne
Petti Varga
*Mona Vaughn
Velvet
Valerie Vogelie
*Violet Vogelie
Ceil Von Dell
Betty Wade
Patti Waggin
Rhea Walker
Bea Ware
*Betty Ware

Beverly Ware, "The Buzz Bomb"
Bunny Ware
Hinda Wassau
"Kiss-Me-On-The-Boo Boo" Watson
*Norma Jean Watts
Trudy Wayne
Vicki Welles
Evelyn "Treasure Chest" West
*Mori White
Wava White
Gee Whiz
*Brandy Wilde
*Darbi Wilde
Shimmy Wilde
Gaby Williams
Gale Winds, "The Original Twister"
Lotus Wing
Pat-Z Wolf
Peggy Wood
Leah Wynn, "The Blonde Venus"
Coby Yee
Dallas York
Lynn York
Geni Young
Lonnie Young
Roxy Young
*Yvonne Yvette
Zabouda
ZaZa
Zorima
*Zorita
Zada Zorn
Lady Zorro

Chorus girls on stage performing for the audience at Leon & Eddie's.
PHOTO COURTESY OF: MARINKA.

Chorus girl Elaine Thomas backstage at the Boston Casino Theatre, 1954.
PHOTO COURTESY OF: THE FASCINATING JENNIFER.

Chorus girl Nancy "Babe" Johnson backstage at the Boston Casino Theatre, 1954. PHOTO COURTESY OF: THE FASCINATING JENNIFER.

Chorus girl Peggy Wood posing backstage at the Casino Theatre, Pittsburgh. PHOTO COURTESY OF: JONI TAYLOR.

Joni Taylor and Peggy Wood sweeping the stage between performances at the Casino Theatre in Pittsburgh, 1955. PHOTO COURTESY OF: JONI TAYLOR.

Chorus girl Lynn Cammarata, relaxing backstage at the Casino Theatre, Pittsburgh.
PHOTO COURTESY OF: JONI TAYLOR.

Chorus girl Lynn Cammarata with prop reindeer at the Casino Theatre, Pittsburgh.
PHOTO COURTESY OF: JONI TAYLOR.

Chorus girl Helen Jolosky "just clowning around" in the dressing room, backstage at the Casino Theatre, Pittsburgh.
PHOTO COURTESY OF: JONI TAYLOR.

List of Comics & Straight Men

Backstage between shows, Dick Richards and others created a list of people they worked with over the years, preserving a small piece of burlesque history. The list is quite extensive and literally a "Who's Who" in burlesque. By preserving this type of material, we can determine the comics from the straight men.

COMICS

Billy Ainsley
Jack Albertson
Ambark Ali
Al Anger
Billy Arlington
Harry Arnie
Hap Arnold
Lou Ascol
Herbie Barris
Clyde Bates
Irving Benson
Harry Bentley
Dick Bernie
Bert Berry
Freddy "Falls" Binder
Lew Black
Wally Blair
Charles "Peanuts" Bohn
Kenny Brenna

George Broadhurst
Artie Brooks
Lou Brown
Walter "Schultz, the Butcher" Brown
Smokey Burns
Red Buttons
Bob Carney
Bert Carr
Harry Clexx
Cliff Cochran
Max Coleman
Billy Collins
Marty Collins
Harry J. Conley
Lou Costello
Jimmy Coughlin
Charles "Klutz" Country
Joey Cowan

Glen Dale
Pat Daly
Charles "Bimbo" Davis
Eddie Davis
Johnny D'Arco
Mac Dennison
Joe De Rita
Lew Devine
Leon De Voe
Willie Dew
Jack Diamond
Milt Douglas
Jimmy Dugan
Red Dulin
Harry Evanson
Harold Farr
Bobby Faye
Herbie Faye
Joey Faye
Bob Ferguson
Mack Ferguson
Billy Fields
George Fields
Harry "Hello Jake" Fields
Harry "Stinky" Fields
Dusty "Open the Door,
   Richard Fletcher
Billy Foster
Freddie Frampton
Joe Freed
Charles "Haba-Haba" Fritcher
Jack "Tiny" Fuller
Maxie Furman
Art Gardner
Billy "Sneeze" Gilbert
Jackie Gleason
Charlie "Uncle Ezra" Goldie
Abe Gore

Jo-Jo Gostel
Gene Graham
Eddie Green
Bob Greer
Count Gregory
Billy "Cheese 'n' Crackers"
   Hagen
I. B. Hamp
Irving Harmon
George Hart
Gabby Hayes
Will Hays
Hank Henry
George B. Hill
Cress Hillary
Dave Hoffman
Jack Hunt
Happy Hyatt
Eddie Innis
Mickey Jay
Eddie "Nut" Kaplin
Mandy Kaye
Sparky Kaye
Charlie Kemper
Billy King
Johnny "Higgy" King
Manny King
Benny "Beans" Kirkland
Monkey Kirkland
Ray Kolb
Bert Lahr
Jack LaMont
Harry Landers
Charles LaVine
Everett Lawson
Pinky Lee
Harry "Shuffles" LeVan
Harry Levine

Freddie Lewis
George "Beetle puss" Lewis
Harry "Lifty" Lewis
Irvin "Too Soon" Lewis
Lew Lewis
Murray "Looney" Lewis
Little Jack Little
Artie Lloyd
Eddie Lloyd
Bozo Lord
Billy "Bumps" Mack
Dave "Snuffy" Marion
Pigmeat Markham
Bert Marks
Charles "Red" Marshall
Ken Martin
Jimmy Mathews
Claude Mathis
Matty Matthews
Perry Mayo
"Shorty" McAllister
Boob McManus
Charles "Tramp" McNally
Harry "Boob" Meyers
Nat Mercy
Tommy "Scurvy" Miller
Steve Mills
O. P. Mitchell
Jack Montague
Benny "Wop" Moore
Bobby Morris
Joe Morris
Miles K. Murphy
George Murray
Sid "Fuzz" Nadell
Charlie Naples
Buddy O'Day
Walter Owens

Joe "Wanna Buy a Duck?
    Penner
Frank Penny
Jack "Ducknose" Pershing
Al Pharr
Jimmy Pinto
Lou Powers
Garrett Price
Sammy Price
Tommy "Moe" Raft
Rags Ragland
Happy Ray
Sam Raynor
Billy Reed
Abe Reynolds
Dick Richards
Al Rio
Charlie Robinson
Harry Rose
Hermie Rose
Jack Rose
Jimmy "Bubbles" Rose
Joe Rose
Jack Rosen
Joe E. Ross
Mike Sachs
Bozo St. Clair
Harry Savoy
Gus Schilling
Chuck Sexton
Irving Selig
Harry Seymour
Jack Shargel
George Shelton
Harry Siegal
Frank X. Silk
Phil Silvers
Hal Skelly

Red Skelton
Sammy Smith
Tommy "Bozo" Snyder
Jack Sobel
Sammy Spears
Walt Stanford
Harry Steppe
Billy "Bozo" Stone
George Stone
Harry Stratton
Billy Tanner
Virgil "Slats" Taylor
Danny Thomas
Tommy Timlin
Bobby Vail

Earl Van
Harry Vine
Sid Walker
Scratch Wallace
"Sliding" Billy Watson
Art Watts
John Weber
Bobby Wilson
Chuck Wilson
Bob Winkler
Paul "Bozo" Workman
Sam Wright
Ed Wynn
Joe "Hey Hey" Yule

STRAIGHT MEN

Bud Abbott
Robert Alda
Jack Arnold
Chet Atland
Al Baker, Sr.
Harry Beasley
Bob Birch
Mel Bishop
Murray Briscoe
Frank Bryan
Buddy Bryant
Jack Buckley
Walter Budd
Tom Bundy
Pat Burns
Fred Clark
Lee Clifford
Ralph Clifford
Dave Cohn

Walt Collins
Johnny Cook
Jack Coyle
Dick Dana
Matty Della
Lou Denny
Joe Devlin
Dudley Douglas
Lou Duthers
Chick Evans
Danny Evans
Joe Forte
James X. Francis
Milt Frome
Parker Gee
Burt Gehan
Al Golden
John Grant
Murray Green

Floyd Hallicy
Ben Hamilton
Milt Hamilton
Mervin Harmon
Charlie Harris
John Head
Jack Heath
Clyde Hodges
Franklin Hodges
Tom Howard
Chick Hunter
Danny Jacobs
Johnny Kane
Bill E. King
Matt Kolb
Billy Koud
Dick Lancaster
Phil Lane
Tommy Layne
Bob Lee
Johnny LeLong
Murray Leonard
Danny Lewis
Meggs Lexing
Joe Lyons
Hughie Mack
Jess Mack
Lester Mack
Dexter Maitland
Johnny Maloney
Jack Mann
Jack Martin
Wen Miller
Stanley Montfort
Howard Montgomery

Danny Morton
Al Murray
Jack Murray
D. Ray Parsons
Raymond Payne
Harry Peterson
Tom Phillips
Wilbur Rance
Bob Ridley
Bob Rogers
George Rose
Connie Ryan
Harry Ryan
Paul Ryan
Bert Saunders
Ernie Schroeder
Charley Schultz
Phil Seed
Merrill Sevier
George Shaeffer
Wally Sharples
Frank C. Smith
Lee Stuart
Bob Taylor
Mitch Todd
Russell Trent
Danny Tucker
Forrest Tucker
George Tuttle
Johnny Watson
Maurie Wayne
Paul West
Harry White
Joe Wilton
Eddie Yubel

Joey Faye.
PHOTO COURTESY OF: LADY MIDNIGHT.

Billy Arlington.

Bobby Morris, Charles "Red" Marshall, and Phil Silvers—burlesque comics.
PHOTO COURTESY OF: MIMI REED.

BELOW:
Comic Charles "Red" Marshall and straight man Robert Alda.
PHOTO COURTESY OF: MIMI REED.

Above Left:
Charlie Kemper.
Photo courtesy of: Al Baker, Jr.

Above:
Dexter Maitland.
Photo courtesy of: Irving Benson.

Left:
Straight man D. Ray Parsons and Betty Rowland.
Photo courtesy of: Mimi Reed.

Rags Ragland.
PHOTO COURTESY OF: MIMI REED.

Specialty dancer and talking woman Mimi Reed with straight man D. Ray Parsons.
PHOTO COURTESY OF: MIMI REED.

Hank Henry.
PHOTO COURTESY OF: MIMI REED.

Billy Reed.
PHOTO COURTESY OF: MIMI REED.

Mona Vaughn and comic Abe Gore performing on stage at the Moulin Rouge Theatre in Oakland, California in the early 1940s.
PHOTO COURTESY OF: MONA VAUGHN/BURLESQUE HISTORICAL SOCIETY.

Happy Hyatt.
PHOTO COURTESY
OF: MONA
VAUGHN/BURLESQUE
HISTORICAL
SOCIETY.

**Comics Harry Conley and Billy Ainsley backstage at the
Boston Casino Theatre, 1956.**
PHOTO COURTESY OF: THE FASCINATING JENNIFER.

Comic Bob Ferguson backstage at the Casino Theatre in Boston, 1956.
PHOTO COURTESY OF: THE FASCINATING JENNIFER.

Straight man Harry Ryan posing in his dressing room, backstage at the Casino Theatre in Boston, 1956.
PHOTO COURTESY OF: THE FASCINATING JENNIFER.

Straight man Jack Coyle backstage at the Casino Theatre in Boston.
PHOTO COURTESY OF: THE FASCINATING JENNIFER.

Comic Jack Rosen, straight man Al Baker, Sr., and comic Happy Hyatt posing with unknown novelty dancer backstage at the Casino Theatre in Boston.
PHOTO COURTESY OF: THE FASCINATING JENNIFER.

Comics Benny "Wop" Moore and Slats Taylor.
PHOTO COURTESY OF: MIMI REED.

Comic Jack Rosen backstage at the Casino Theatre in Boston.
PHOTO COURTESY OF: THE FASCINATING JENNIFER.

Slats Taylor.
PHOTO COURTESY OF: LORRAINE LEE.

ABOVE LEFT:
Bozo Lord.
PHOTO COURTESY OF:
LORRAINE LEE.

ABOVE RIGHT:
Harry "Lifty" Lewis.
PHOTO COURTESY OF:
BURLESQUE HISTORICAL
SOCIETY.

LEFT:
Clyde Hodges.
PHOTO COURTESY OF:
LORRAINE LEE.

Strip/talking woman Jean Carroll and comic Walter Owens on stage performing a comedy bit.
Photo courtesy of: Burlesque Historical Society.

Billy King.
PHOTO COURTESY OF: BURLESQUE
HISTORICAL SOCIETY.

Billy King on stage.
PHOTO COURTESY OF: PAT
ELLIOTT MINSKY/BURLESQUE
HISTORICAL SOCIETY.

Steve Mills.
PHOTO COURTESY OF: PAT ELLIOTT
MINSKY/BURLESQUE HISTORICAL
SOCIETY.

Monkey Kirkland.
PHOTO COURTESY OF: PAT ELLIOTT
MINSKY/BURLESQUE HISTORICAL
SOCIETY.

TOMMY "MOE" RAFT

Tommy "Moe" Raft.
Photo courtesy of: Pat Elliott Minsky/Burlesque Historical Society.

Straight man Ralph Clifford and comic Jimmy Mathews.
PHOTO COURTESY OF: PAT ELLIOTT MINSKY/BURLESQUE HISTORICAL SOCIETY.

Irving Benson.
PHOTO COURTESY OF: PAT ELLIOTT MINSKY/BURLESQUE HISTORICAL SOCIETY.

Jimmy Pinto, 1957.
PHOTO COURTESY OF: JONI TAYLOR.

Backstage, Minsky Show, at the Dunes Hotel in Las Vegas, Nevada. From Left to Right: Straight man Dick Dana, comic Irving Benson, Eddie Lynch—stage manager at the Dunes, and a part of the Harold Minsky organization for 20 years, and comics Joe De Rita and Tommy "Moe" Raft.
Photo courtesy of: Pat Elliott Minsky/Burlesque Historical Society.

Straight man Lee Clifford and talking woman Barbara Curtis backstage at the Roxy Theatre in Cleveland, Ohio, 1958.
PHOTO COURTESY OF: BARBARA CURTIS AND JONI TAYLOR.

Comic Jack Rosen backstage in Baltimore, 1954.
PHOTO COURTESY OF: JONI TAYLOR.

Al Anger.
PHOTO COURTESY OF: BARBARA CURTIS AND JONI TAYLOR.

ABOVE:
Barbara Curtis and Lou Brown performing together on stage, 1946.
PHOTO COURTESY OF: BARBARA CURTIS AND JONI TAYLOR.

RIGHT:
Barbara Curtis and Al Anger, 1964.
PHOTO COURTESY OF: BARBARA CURTIS AND JONI TAYLOR.

ABOVE LEFT:
Comics Bob Ferguson and Jack Rosen, 1957.
PHOTO COURTESY OF: JONI TAYLOR.

ABOVE RIGHT:
Comic Al Anger, straight man Lee Clifford, and comic Artie Lloyd, 1957.
PHOTO COURTESY OF: BARBARA CURTIS AND JONI TAYLOR.

LEFT:
Comic Joey Cowan, straight man Harry White, and comic Al Anger, 1954.
PHOTO COURTESY OF: BARBARA CURTIS AND JONI TAYLOR.

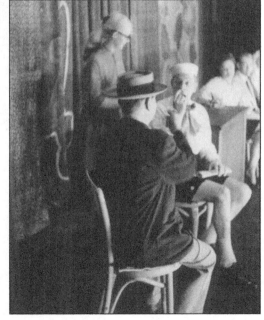

School Room Scene, from the wings. From left to right: Al Anger, Barbara Curtis, Artie Lloyd, Joanne Dimples, unknown, and Sigried Fox.
PHOTOS COURTESY OF: BARBARA CURTIS AND JONI TAYLOR.

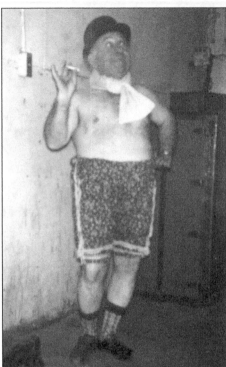

LEFT:
Comic Little Jack Little clowning around backstage at the Gayety Theatre in Toledo, Ohio.
PHOTO COURTESY OF: LEE STUART.

BELOW LEFT:
Comic Little Jack Little and dancer Theodora "just having some fun" backstage at the Gayety Theatre, in Toledo, Ohio.
PHOTO COURTESY OF: LEE STUART.

BELOW:
Burlesque front advertising Little Jack Little, Lee Stuart, and Ray Kolb, at the Gayety Theatre in Toledo, Ohio.
PHOTO COURTESY OF: LEE STUART.

Comic Little Jack Little and straight man Lee Stuart outside the Gayety Theatre, in Toledo, Ohio.
PHOTO COURTESY OF: LEE STUART.

Straight man Lee Stuart in front of the Rivoli Theatre in Seattle, Washington.
PHOTO COURTESY OF: LEE STUART.

LEFT:
Comic Chuck Sexton and straight man Lee Stuart.
PHOTO COURTESY OF: LEE STUART.

BELOW:
Lee Stuart and Chuck Sexton off stage.
PHOTO COURTESY OF: LEE STUART.

RIGHT:
Comic Earl Van in front of the Gayety Theatre in Toledo, Ohio.
PHOTO COURTESY OF: LEE STUART.

BELOW:
Comic Phil McCabe working on a costume backstage at the Empress Theatre in Milwaukee, Wisconsin.
PHOTO COURTESY OF: LEE STUART.

BELOW RIGHT:
Comics Monkey Kirkland and Ray Kolb "monkeying around" backstage at the Gayety Theatre in Toledo, Ohio.
PHOTO COURTESY OF: LEE STUART.

Comic Bert Berry backstage at the Gayety Theatre in Toledo, Ohio.
PHOTO COURTESY OF: LEE STUART.

Comic Hermie Rose "moving in" to the Rivoli Theatre in Seattle, Washington.
PHOTO COURTESY OF: LEE STUART.

Comic Walter Brown and straight man Lee Stuart.
PHOTO COURTESY OF: LEE STUART.

Straight man Lee Stuart and comic Walter Brown.
PHOTO COURTESY OF: LEE STUART.

Comics Earl Van and Ray Kolb backstage at the Gayety Theatre in Toledo, Ohio.
PHOTO COURTESY OF: LEE STUART.

Posing outside the Gayety Theatre in Toledo, Ohio, from left to right: stagehand Tish, comic Ray Kolb, dancer Ann Curtis, and comic Earl Van.
PHOTO COURTESY OF: LEE STUART.

Comics Ray Kolb and Sammy Price spending time with Sam's son Mark, before preparing for their next show.
PHOTO COURTESY OF: LEE STUART.

Performers in a comedy bit on stage at the Rivoli Theatre in Seattle, include comic Johnny "Higgy" King and straight man Lee Stuart.
PHOTO COURTESY OF: LEE STUART.

On stage at the Rivoli Theatre in Seattle, from left to right: comic Johnny "Higgy" King, unknown player, straight man Lee Stuart, Elaine Stuart, and another unknown player.
PHOTO COURTESY OF: LEE STUART.

Comic Tommy "Bozo" Snyder, with no stage make-up.
Photo courtesy of: Lee Stuart.

Comic Tommy "Bozo" Snyder all made up; ready to perform.
Photo courtesy of: Lee Stuart.

Straight man Lee Stuart and comic Hermie Rose.
PHOTO COURTESY OF: LEE STUART.

Straight man Lee Stuart and comic Charlie Goldie performing on stage.
PHOTO COURTESY OF: LEE STUART.

Jack La Mont; one of those guys who could work as either a comic or straight man.
PHOTO COURTESY OF: LEE STUART.

Ray Kolb.
PHOTO COURTESY OF: LEE STUART.

Comic George "Bozo" Lord in street clothes.
PHOTO COURTESY OF: LEE STUART.

Old friends, comics George "Bozo" Lord and Ray Kolb, posing for a photograph behind the theatre.
PHOTO COURTESY OF: LEE STUART.

Paul West and Meggs Lexing.
PHOTO COURTESY OF: LEE STUART.

ABOVE:
Jim West, Nat Mercy, Ray Kolb, and Kathie Kelly; after performing a comedy bit called "Duffy's Daughter Kate."
PHOTO COURTESY OF: LEE STUART.

RIGHT:
Comic Ray Kolb, dressed in civvies, standing in front of the theatre and next to a sign advertising Toni Rave.
PHOTO COURTESY OF: LEE STUART.

Scene from famous old burlesque bit "Crazy House."
PHOTO COURTESY OF: LEE STUART.

Performing on stage, straight man Charlie Crafts, comic Eddie Ware, and "The Bazoom Girl," Jennie Lee.
PHOTO COURTESY OF: PAT FLANNERY.

In a 1978 handwritten letter which accompanied this photo, Looney Lewis explained to Pat Elliott Minsky, "Am sending the only photo of myself on stage. The rest I lost in a fire." (The woman was not identified.)
Photo courtesy of: Pat Elliott Minsky/Burlesque Historical Society.

Comics Irving Benson and Joey Cowan.
Photo courtesy of: Vivi Lynn.

Comic Scurvy Miller and friend Mary, backstage in Chicago.
Photo courtesy of: Vivi Lynn.

Posing backstage for a photograph, straight man Floyd Hallicy and comic Billy "Cheese 'n' Crackers" Hagen.
PHOTO COURTESY OF: VIVI LYNN.

Comic Ray Kolb clowning in his backyard.
PHOTOS COURTESY OF: LEE STUART.

Straight man Danny Jacobs, comic Dick Richards, and talking woman Barbara Curtis.
Photo courtesy of: Pat Elliott Minsky/Burlesque Historical Society.

Working the car scene bit, from left to right: Pat Flannery, Charlie Crafts, "unknown comic," and Doreen Gray. Help us identify the "unknown comic."
PHOTO COURTESY OF: BURLESQUE HISTORICAL SOCIETY.

Another shot of the car scene . . . including an "unknown comic." From left to right: Doreen Gray, Charlie Crafts, Pat Flannery, and the "unknown comic."
PHOTO COURTESY OF: BURLESQUE HISTORICAL SOCIETY.

ABOVE:
Straight man Matt Kolb's promotional postcard.
PHOTO COURTESY OF: LEE STUART.

LEFT:
Comic Wally Blair.
PHOTO COURTESY OF: ROSEMARIE "SEPTEMBER ROSE" HARMON.

ABOVE:
Comic Jimmy Mathews.
PHOTO COURTESY OF:
DAVID HANSON.

RIGHT:
Comic Claude Mathis.
PHOTO COURTESY OF:
DAVID HANSON.

Comic Lou Ascol.

Jimmy Mathews, Claude Mathis and Buddy Graf.
PHOTO COURTESY OF: DAVID HANSON.

Comic Benny "Wop" Moore.
PHOTO COURTESY OF: BURLESQUE
HISTORICAL SOCIETY.

Comic Benny "Wop" Moore.
PHOTO COURTESY OF: BURLESQUE
HISTORICAL SOCIETY.

Comic Benny "Wop" Moore.
PHOTO COURTESY OF: BURLESQUE
HISTORICAL SOCIETY.

Comic Benny "Wop" Moore.
PHOTO COURTESY OF: BURLESQUE
HISTORICAL SOCIETY.

Comic Benny "Wop" Moore.
PHOTO COURTESY OF: BURLESQUE HISTORICAL SOCIETY.

Comic Benny "Wop" Moore.
PHOTO COURTESY OF: BURLESQUE HISTORICAL SOCIETY.

Straight man and agent Jess Mack.
PHOTO COURTESY OF: BURLESQUE
HISTORICAL SOCIETY.

Eddie Lloyd.
PHOTO COURTESY OF: BURLESQUE
HISTORICAL SOCIETY.

Comic Al Rio.
PHOTO COURTESY OF: BURLESQUE
HISTORICAL SOCIETY.

Al Rio.
PHOTO COURTESY OF: BURLESQUE
HISTORICAL SOCIETY.

Hal Webber.

Jack Martin.

**Half of the team Stanley and
Donato; Stanley was the comic.**

**The other half of team Stanley and
Donato; Donato was the straight man.**

Stanley and Donato.

ABOVE LEFT:
Billy Fields.
PHOTO COURTESY OF:
BURLESQUE HISTORICAL
SOCIETY.

ABOVE:
Billy "Cheese N' Crackers" Hagen.
PHOTO COURTESY OF:
BURLESQUE HISTORICAL
SOCIETY.

LEFT:
Fred Binder.
PHOTO COURTESY OF:
BURLESQUE HISTORICAL
SOCIETY.

Claude Mathis.
PHOTO COURTESY OF: BURLESQUE HISTORICAL SOCIETY.

ABOVE LEFT:
Jack Maloney.
PHOTO COURTESY OF:
BURLESQUE HISTORICAL
SOCIETY.

ABOVE:
Parker Gee.
PHOTO COURTESY OF:
BURLESQUE HISTORICAL
SOCIETY.

LEFT:
Mack Ferguson.
PHOTO COURTESY OF: NORMA
JEAN & ART WATTS
FAMILY/BURLESQUE HISTORICAL
SOCIETY COLLECTION.

Gene Graham; comic and emcee.
Photo courtesy of: Norma Jean & Art Watts Family/Burlesque Historical Society Collection.